FOR

NORMAL

by

Darcy Pattison

Mims House, Little Rock, AR

Mims House
1309 Broadway
Little Rock, AR 72202
www.mimshouse.com

Publisher's Cataloging-in-Publication data

Pattison, Darcy. 1954-

p. cm.

Summary: A boy unites an immigrant community and rebuilds his family–using a simple sourdough bread recipe.

Longing for Normal/by Darcy Pattison

Hardcover 978-1-62944-041-5

Paperback 978-1-62944-042-2

eBook 978-1-62944-043-9

1. Family life—Fiction 2. Schools–Fiction 3. Family problems—Fiction I. Pattison, Darcy II. Longing for Normal

Library of Congress Control Number: 2014918923
Printed in the United States of America

For Haileigh, Bruce, Zeke and Gabe.
You make family something special
.

BEFORE THE BREAD PROJECT BEGINS

ELIOT

Ba-boom, ba-boom, ba-boom.

Standing outside the gymnasium doors, a drumbeat throbbed. Yellow light streamed from the second story windows. I couldn't hear the music's melody, just the drum beat: ba-boom, ba-boom.

The Back-to-School party at Wilma Rudolph Elementary School had already started.

I reached for the door handle, but Marj, my almost-adoptive-mother put a hand on my shoulder. Her hand trembled. "Don't leave me alone in there," she said.

I understood: Dad and I had been at this school for the past six years and she was the new one here. "I know," I said.

I took a deep breath and hauled open the heavy door. Marj lifted her chin and entered.

Following her inside, I heard someone yell: "Eliot Winston! Oh, you poor boy. Come here."

I winced.

There she was, that Mrs. Lopez. Her voice could cut through anything, even concrete. She sat beside a poster that read: "Back to School Party! Join the PTA Here!" Another poster said: "Support your PTA! School T-shirts, only $5."

No way to avoid Mrs. Lopez, she wouldn't let you. I led Marj toward the PTA table, but that was a problem. Because I had a mission: the Bread Project had to be toast. And I had a plan: talk Mrs. Lopez into talking everyone else into dropping the Bread Project. It should be simple, except I had to talk to Mrs. Lopez without Marj listening in.

Mrs. Lopez met us halfway from the door and pulled me into a bear hug. "Poor boy!"

I swallowed hard and pulled back, so I wouldn't get thrown off-balance.

But I was off-balance, just walking into the school building. Tonight, I had to figure out how to be back at school and be okay.

"Ah, *mi amigo*." Mrs. Lopez stepped back and held my shoulders at arm's length. "It's been a long summer, *sí*?"

Turmoil bubbled up inside: this was not the time nor place, though. I looked past her, trying to get a grip on my emotions. I made myself study the three aisles of game booths. Someone had made palm trees out of the poles that hold the volleyball nets and then stuck the fake trees at the front of each aisle. Little kids crowded onto the tire base of each pole, shoving and laughing. On one tire, though, a skinny girl sat alone. She was older, maybe fourth or fifth grade, and just sat there, eating blue cotton candy.

Mrs. Lopez stepped aside. "This is *tu madre*, your mother?"

My heart went skippety-skip. A sideways glance: Marj's freckles looked friendly enough, even if she wasn't smiling. But she didn't answer the question, didn't say she was my mother.

My throat tightened, so I could only squeak, "Mrs. Lopez, this is Marj Winston. Marj, this is Mrs. Lopez. President of the PTA."

To see Mrs. Lopez's smile was to understand the amazing abilities of a mouth. Her mouth was as wide as Shamu-the-whale's, and everyone knew her business—including every one of her silver fillings. Nothing was private. She was nothing like Marj.

Two weeks ago, Marj came home with her long fly-away hair all cut off. "Precision cut," Marj said, as if soldiering her hair would put the rest of our lives back in order. To me, Marj still looked like rumpled laundry.

"Finally," Mrs. Lopez said. "I'm so glad to meet Griff's widow. Such a sad thing."

Mrs. Lopez never avoided a subject but waded right in. She had almost thrown me off a minute before, but it was the right thing for Marj. Because there was Marj's hand, ready to shake. She even curved her lips into an almost smile, like the thumping music had loosened her frozen face. I guess Marj needed people to be honest.

"Yes, I'm Mrs. Winston. I've heard lots of good things about you."

"Oh, that Griff." Mrs. Lopez laughed and waved a hand. "Always talking about school. I bet you know something about everyone here. You know all our secrets, *sí*?"

Marj lifted an eyebrow, "Perhaps."

And Mrs. Lopez laughed.

Now that they were introduced, I remembered my mission: "Excuse me. Mrs. Lopez, could I talk to you about–"

"About what?" she interrupted.

I glanced at Marj, uncertain. What was she thinking about? Was she still nervous about meeting people, about being here at the school where Griff had worked?

"Do I need to go away, so you can talk?" Marj asked.

Mrs. Lopez said, "No, no! I'll talk to Eliot later. First, there are some people who have been wanting to meet you." Mrs. Lopez must have seen my aggravation, because she added, "You understand, right, Eliot?"

Marj shrugged a question at me. Was this okay?

I sucked on my bottom lip, angry with myself. I really needed to talk with Mrs. Lopez alone. I should've known Mrs. Lopez would grab Marj right away. It was like I had forgotten everything I ever knew about people at school. And would Marj be mad if I insisted on talking to Mrs. Lopez? Maybe. I didn't know.

I shrugged back at Marj. "Sure. We can meet people first."

"You go on and look for your friends," Marj said encouragingly. "I'll be fine."

"What?" I blinked. "You just told me not to leave you alone." And here she was taking off with a stranger to meet other strangers. And she was going to be fine?

Before Marj could answer, Mrs. Lopez put an arm around her shoulder and said, "She changed her mind. When you lose your husband, well, it's hard to think, hard to make decisions for a while."

Marj nodded, agreeing with her.

I just stared from one to the other, amazed. But then I looked again: Under the bright lights of the gymnasium, Marj's eyes were pale smudges of blue-gray. Last night, when everything was dark and quiet in the house, I had heard her crying. Neither of us was sleeping well.

Mrs. Lopez continued, "Of course, she was scared coming in. She didn't know us. But Griff told us all about her. She has *amigos* already, she just has to meet them." She pulled Marj tighter, into a protective hug.

Throwing up my hands, I shook my head. Maybe I did understand a little bit, maybe it was okay. But I had to try again with Mrs. Lopez: "Please, I just need one minute to talk to you. About the Bread Project–"

"Ah, that." Her brow furrowed, then cleared. "There's time for that later, *mi amigo*. Find me later." Mrs. Lopez's easy-going ways were almost impossible to argue with.

I opened my mouth. Then shut it. I did want Marj and Mrs. Lopez to talk and be friends. I did want Mrs. Lopez to introduce Marj around. But I didn't want them to talk about the Bread Project. Now that I'd been dumb enough to mention it, though, they probably would. "Sure," I said. "I'll find you later."

Mentally, I shifted gears: "Say, have you seen Toby tonight?"

"Si. He's here somewhere," Mrs. Lopez said.

Despite everything, I felt a small thrill. School was starting, and Toby and I were in sixth grade, the oldest. The leaders.

Another PTA mom took over the membership table. "Take a long break if you need," she told Mrs. Lopez.

Figuring they were done with me, I turned toward the booths and came face-to-face with a scrawny girl who came out of nowhere–she startled me. Her lips were blue, blue from eating cotton candy. Stumbling back, I mumbled, "Sorry."

Mrs. Lopez said, "Eliot, this is Alli. She's new, and she's sixth grade, like you. Can she go around with you and Toby?"

ALLI

Mr. Porter dumped me just inside the front door of the gymnasium.

He walked in, saw this woman and said, "Mrs. Lopez, I have to work the game outside. Can you keep an eye on Alli? You heard she's staying with us for a while?"

Mrs. Lopez leaned over and pulled a stack of shirts out of a large box. "Your first try at a foster child, *sí*?" She shook out a tiny shirt–must have been an XXX-small–and folded it, while Mr. Porter introduced me to her.

"Si, leave her to me." Mrs. Lopez pointed at some fake palm trees. "Sit over there for now." She shook out another shirt and started smoothing it flat. "When things calm down," she said, "maybe we can walk around."

"Can't I walk around by myself?" I protested.

Mr. Porter winced. My voice had that effect on some people. Talk softer, some said to me. But that didn't help, my voice was just rough.

Mr. Porter said, "No, you can't go around alone. Not your first week with us. The state says someone has to be watching you."

I frowned, irritated at being treated like a child. But I finally shrugged, realizing that there was no fighting the red-tape. I'd just wait until Mrs. Lopez was busy, and then I'd look around.

"Thanks," Mr. Porter said to Mrs. Lopez. "You need anything else?"

"No, you helped enough, getting all the tables set up, carrying in all our boxes. *Gracias.*" Mr. Porter shot me a last order: "Don't wander off, Alli. Make sure Mrs. Lopez knows where you are. I'll be outside, in back. Have a good time." Then he walked off, energetic-like, with his hands in his jeans pockets.

And there I was. Alone.

So what? I could take care of myself.

Volleyball poles and construction paper leaves–what a sad palm tree. But the base of the pole was a tire, a decent place to sit. I dug into the pocket of my school uniform, found the money from Miss Porter, Mr. Porter's sister, bought blue cotton candy and sat down. To watch. To get an idea of what this place was like.

Families started to trickle in. Mostly little kids. But now and then someone who might be in my grade, sixth grade. At my old school, I was supposed to be the spelling bee champ this year, supposed to be with my friends for one last year before moving up–instead, I had to change schools. And the first day here, I was abandoned.

Abandoned: Latin derivation: Forsaken or deserted. A-b-a-n-d-o-n-e-d.

Would sixth grade be easy at this school? How long would I be here? Where would I be for the seventh grade? Seemed like all I ever did was ask questions that had no answers. Like, was Mandy okay?

"Eliot Winston!"

I winced at the loud voice and missed the rest of what was said. I didn't miss who said it, though, Mrs. Lopez. Over her other clothes, she had pulled on a school T-shirt in an awful shade of green. "Perfectly dreadful color," as Mrs. Ferguson, the art teacher from my old school would have said.

Mrs. Lopez marched up to a skinny boy, then grabbed and hugged him. Like a pit bull clamping down on a Chihuahua puppy. I guessed he was the fourth or fifth grade. Finally, the boy–Eliot, she called him–squirmed loose.

'Course I didn't mean to eavesdrop, but then nobody ever notices me.

"Really, just one minute," Eliot said. "About the Bread Project, just one–"

Bread Project? What was that? The boy acted like he didn't want his mom to know about it. Was it something important at this school?

I stood and stretched and thought I'd walk around now that Mrs. Lopez was busy with that kid. Over by the door, huddling like they were afraid to move, were two girls wearing head scarves. Probably the new girls from the Herat family. When I registered for school yesterday, the counselor was talking about them. About the Kurdish family with nieces coming in soon. About this neighborhood, south Nashville, which had people from over 40 nations. Kurds, Somalians, Sudanese, Egyptians, Arabs, Indians, and lots of Hispanics from lots of South American countries. The counselor had a world map on her wall with pins stuck in it. Her third year at the school, she said, and she couldn't believe immigrants were still coming in so fast.

Just then, the gym doors pushed open, and a tall, dark-skinned boy entered, followed by his mom in a bright red sari. An Indian family, I guessed. Or Pakistani. Or something. The door almost slammed on the mother, and she reached out to jerk an earplug from the boy's ear.

"And keep that off so you can hear me," she scolded. At the PTA table, she picked up a green T-shirt and held it to the boy's back. "What size are you wearing now?"

Mothers. They had a hard time keeping track of things. Like changing shirt sizes. And allowances. I patted the last dollar in my pocket. Mom and Dad–

–no, Mandy and Ted. I had to remember not to call them Mom and Dad any more.

Mandy and Ted had given me an allowance from the monthly state support check. But I'd heard stories about some foster parents who kept all the check to themselves. Mr. Porter had just frowned when I'd asked for money tonight. But then Miss Porter had pulled out two dollars, so he hadn't said anything for sure.

"Alli Flynn!"

Mrs. Lopez was motioning to me. Oh, great. So much for looking around on my own. I strolled over. Just as I got to the PTA table, Eliot spun around—

Hey! Were those arms or long pieces of spaghetti slapping at my face? "Look out!" I yelled.

He jerked back and mumbled, "Sorry."

He was skinny and had brown hair.

Mrs. Lopez said, "Eliot, this is Alli. She's new, and she's sixth grade, like you. She needs someone to show her around. Can she go around with you and Toby?"

Eliot looked me up and down.

Mr. Porter had bought me used school uniforms before he even saw me, assuming I'd be the size of an average sixth grader instead of an average fifth grader. Okay, fourth grader, maybe. And then, he made me wear the uniform tonight.

Eliot said, "You can't be sixth grade. You're too little."

We were about the same height: he was just an inch taller, so I didn't see why he wanted to be insulting. But I said nothing. Too much trouble.

To Mrs. Lopez, Eliot said, "Whatever."

"Eliot!" his mother said. "You know better."

Mrs. Lopez nodded approval at his mom.

Eliot didn't look at me. Just frowned, and said, "Yes, ma'am. She can go with us."

Mrs. Lopez led Eliot's mom toward a group of parents.

Eliot walked past me and I threw the paper cone–all that was left of the cotton candy–into the blue trash barrel and followed. Ignoring me, he walked on tiptoe, trying to see over the crowd. His head swiveled back and forth apparently searching for someone.

No luck on the first aisle.

Suddenly, he shoved forward down the middle aisle, like he was afraid someone would disappear. He glanced back to see if I was following, dodged two clusters of foreign-looking people, and kept going.

I kept up: he couldn't lose me. Not till I wanted to be lost.

Eliot stopped in front of a group of white-blond kids. "Toby!"

Five turquoise T-shirts stared at Eliot. No, six. Even the mother wore a turquoise T-shirt and jean shorts. They didn't need to dress alike, not with that white-blond hair. They looked crazy, like identical Easter Eggs.

The mother headed straight for Eliot and wrapped him in a turquoise hug. "You poor, precious boy!"

Well, I felt sorry for him, too. Did every adult think they needed to hug him like that? And why were they doing that? What had happened to make him so–well, so precious?

He was faster at getting out of the hug this time. The oldest boy just shrugged at Eliot. That must be Toby.

The mother finally turned loose and stared at me. "And who is this?"

"New girl, sixth grade," Eliot said. "Name's Alli." To me, he said, "Alli, this is Mrs. Zane. And her kids."

I nodded to Mrs. Zane and reached out to shake her hand. But the smallest blond kid, a girl with short, straight hair, dashed away, arms stretched up and yelling, "Ba-Woon!"

Sure enough, the girl's red balloon floated upward. There, bumping along the ceiling, were a half dozen other balloons.

"Veronica!" The mother chased the girl down and grabbed her hand. "We'll get you a new balloon."

The mother saw me watching. I nodded up at the floating balloons and shook my head in sympathy. She smiled back, and then scooped up her daughter.

Veronica's red balloon reminded me of another balloon, a big one. Ted, my foster father–my old foster father, I reminded myself–was a hot air balloonist. His balloon was totally huge, tomato red, and totally wonderful. The first time I saw it was my first day at Mandy and Ted's house. First grade. We drove out to a field somewhere, and Ted laid out the balloon in the grass. As it inflated, I shouted, I ran around it, I patted it, and finally, I stood frozen, awed, as it stretched up, up, up. When it was fully inflated, I begged for a ride.

That first time five years ago, I couldn't see over the top of the basket. Ted held me up, tight and safe. We stared at the silent world below us. Cotton fields, rice fields. And he pointed out the school in the distance and explained that was where I would go the next day.

Now? Mandy was expecting her own daughter, except things weren't going so good. Mandy was on complete bed rest. I tried to help, bringing up a tray with a snack of cheese and crackers.

But through the bedroom door, I heard Ted saying, "We agreed. We had a good home and there were kids who needed a safe place."

"But you never wanted to adopt." I could imagine the way Mandy's hand would flutter toward him, the way it always did when he disagreed with her.

There was a long silence.

"We didn't know it would take so long for me to get pregnant," Mandy said.

"Alli has been safe with us," Ted said, as if reassuring himself. "Happy."

"For a long time," Mandy agreed.

"How much more would anyone expect us to do?"

"You're the one who never wanted to adopt, you said that." Mandy said. "Alli was only supposed to be here until we had our own baby."

And I felt like I had been stabbed. I had to grip the tray hard so it wouldn't fall. I leaned against the wall and slid to the floor. Behind the door, there was just silence. I could imagine Mandy's hand resting on the bump in her belly, the baby they both wanted.

"We did agree." Ted's voice was cold. Just like his heart.

I had left the tray outside the bedroom and fled to my room.

I coughed now, burying the words, blocking the memory.

A booth across the aisle caught my attention. I stared at yellow duckies floating in a plastic swimming pool, and tried to calm my breathing.

"Just a nickel!" said the adult working that booth. He wore yellow gloves, I guess to keep his hands dry. "For a nickel you can pick up any duck you want. We'll see if a prize is written on the bottom."

The prizes–stuffed animals and plastic toys–crowded the shelf above the pool.

I backed away, whispering, "No. I'll just watch."

A family strolled over to try their luck. Identical twins, dark-haired boys, each handed over a nickel. Julio and Juan, the parents called them.

Juan won, but Julio didn't. 'Course, that started a fight, so they had to try again. More nickels.

Calmer now, I leaned on the corner of the booth and listened. Eliot was saying, "Mrs. Zane, could I talk to you for a minute?"

"Sure, honey. What do you need?"

"Could you talk to Marj? About the Bread Project–"

"She doesn't know if she wants to do it?" Mrs. Zane said.

There was that Bread Project thing again, what was it? I glanced back at the yellow duckies. Julio and Juan had both won this time, and they high-fived.

"Right," Eliot said, and his voice was tense, like this was something important. "And–"

But Mrs. Zane wasn't listening. The three middle brothers were throwing balls at milk bottles, while Toby cheered for them.

Absently, she said, “The Project is a great idea, isn’t it? Perfect, in fact.”

“No!” Eliot said. “I don’t think–”

Then the smallest blond boy knocked over all his milk bottles, and Mrs. Zane put her fingers to her mouth, and boy, did she whistle.

That whistle, so shrill and piercing. It was so loud the whole gym got quiet.

Ba-boom, ba-boom, the drumbeat from the loud speaker’s music filled the silence.

An aisle away, but still easy to hear, someone said, “Just the Zany Zanes again.”

To my surprise, Mrs. Zane laughed. “The Zany Zanes, that’s us.”

Smiling, I said, “The Mighty Whistler.”

“No,” Mrs. Zane said, “just a mom with a lot of hot air.”

I laughed, making Veronica squirm in her mother’s arms, twisting to see who was laughing.

Which made me laugh even more.

Veronica’s face lit up, the balloon finally forgotten, and she was laughing with me.

By now, the Zane brothers were racing around the corner to start down the next aisle. Quickly, Mrs. Zane followed the trail of three blond tornadoes. Just before she disappeared, she called back, “Don’t worry, Eliot. I’ll talk to Marj, and we’ll get the Bread Project going.”

Left behind in peace, Toby said, “Thought you didn’t like the Bread Project.”

“I don’t,” Eliot said. “Marj says it will honor Griff’s memory. But it was his idea and without him–” Eliot tilted his head back and looked at the balloons that still bounced on the ceiling. His voice quivered, “Without Griff, what’s the point? With him gone, well, I just want to be left alone. To make it through this school year by myself, my way. No one poking around, asking me how I’m feeling. It’s private.” He squeezed his eyes tight and whispered, “It feels so private it’s hard to even SAY that it’s private. Don’t want my business out there like this whole Project would make it.” He shook his head and looked at Toby then. “But your Mom won’t listen. Mrs. Lopez won’t listen.”

"No one really listens till you hit 40 years old." Toby shrugged. "So, just try Mrs. Lopez again later."

Eliot coughed and rubbed his eyes, and I worried that he might cry right there. Instead, he sighed. "Yeah, later."

I stepped forward, curious now. "What is the Bread Project?"

They both jerked around at the sound of my voice.

"Well." Eliot pushed his hair off his forehead. "It's a fund raiser for the school, an idea my dad had." He stopped and blinked.

Toby finished it: "But his Dad's not here; he died this summer. Someone else needs to think of a fund raiser and not use his idea."

Eliot looked away. Casually, like he didn't care about anything, he waved at the booths around us. "It's the same baby games we get every year."

So, he didn't want to talk about it. I understood that: I had things I didn't want to talk about either.

He was right about the games: knock down the milk jars, throw beanbags into a lion's mouth, and guess which cup had the ball.

"Like every other school party," I agreed.

Toby asked, "You been outside yet?"

"Nope," said Eliot.

"They set up one of those water games, where you throw a baseball at a target and–" Toby's eyes gleamed, "–if it hits bull's eye, it dumps someone into a tank of water."

Now that made me mad. Mr. Porter dumped me off instead of asking if I wanted to see the most interesting game at the party. He was probably even in charge of that game and didn't tell me about it, just left me with Mrs. Lopez. And Mrs. Lopez dumped me off on Eliot and Toby. Well, she wasn't here now, and I didn't have to pretend to like these boys any more. "Go on," I said. "I'll come out later." As soon as they left, I'd go outside by myself.

Eliot didn't have to pretend to like me, either. "Sure. See you later."

They walked away.

And there I was again, alone.

So what? I could still take care of myself.

ELIOT

"Who's getting dunked in the water game?" I asked.

"Teachers. PTA. Even Mr. Benton," Toby said.

To hide my grin, I started walking toward the back doors. Over my shoulder, I said, casually, "Bet you can't hit the target and drop someone into the water."

Toby caught me and spun me around. "Bet I can."

I waited, relieved that Toby had taken my bait. He was a good baseball pitcher, just not as strong as adults, so he had a shot at winning.

Toby rocked from heel to toe, toe to heel and stuck out his chest. "I've got ten dollars that says I can hit that target. Standard terms."

Our standard terms meant that for every five dollars I lost, I did an hour of mowing at his dad's apartments for him. Not that I lost often. Most of the time, I helped Toby mow anyway, just so he'd get done faster. Losing didn't change much for me.

But ten dollars wasn't enough: I crossed my arms.

"OK, twenty," Toby said.

I was hoping for more than that. Starting school, I needed lots of cash. Marj had bought me school uniforms, some supplies. But lunch money, socks, I'd have to do on my own, so I wouldn't have to bother her. And pencils. I always push hard when I write and break pencil leads, so I go through them fast.

When I didn't say anything, Toby's chest puffed out even more, and he said, "It costs a dollar for three baseballs."

"I'll pay for the balls."

"OK. Twenty-five."

"Done." I slapped Toby's hand, and we headed outside. "If you can't drop someone into the water with just three balls, you owe me. If you do drop them, I owe you five hours of mowing."

This summer, when Toby and I started betting about everything, I had learned. Repeat the bet exactly. Otherwise, Toby would argue, and I'd get nothing. We both knew what was going on, of course. Toby is a friend, but we both have our pride: he couldn't just hand over cash, I had to earn it.

We stopped at the back door where the school buses unloaded. Without meaning to, I looked down the south hallway. It was silent.

Toby looked straight ahead. "Been back to Griff's office yet?"

"Nope." I was struck by a wave of sadness so deep there were no words for it. I laid my palm on the concrete block wall, needing the reassurance of something solid. The hallway stretched away into darkness.

Quietly, Toby pulled open the door and stepped outside. A warm breeze blew in. I shivered, appreciating that he left me alone. He had no idea how empty, how hollow I felt. No one could know. It felt like a heavy stone of misery had been crammed inside a tiny bottle that was squeezed inside a fist so tight that no one could pry it open.

They couldn't do that Bread Project, they couldn't.

Oh, I knew that people wanted to talk about Griff, wanted to share stories. Everyone knew him; everyone loved him. So, I had started a website about Griff's life and sent messages about it to people on his email list. They were sending in old pictures or writing stories about him. That was a public face, and I could deal with it because on the Internet you can hold people at an arm's length. And you could keep it secret from Marj and your teachers–at least for a while. I just couldn't do the Bread Project here, not at the school where I would have to deal with it every day.

I'd talk to Mrs. Lopez again tonight, and this time, she had to listen. I took a deep breath, then another, until I was calmer and could follow Toby outside.

In the parking lot, the water tank sat under a bright streetlight, surrounded by a low fence to keep people back a ways. So, here's where the fifth and sixth graders had hidden. Brad Garcia, Kinesha Johnson, and a dozen or so other sixth graders were watching. Good. The only way to push back the sadness was to stay busy. Lots of people and lots of action were very good.

I jerked my head away from the crowd and stared at the tank. "Who's on the dunking board? Can you see?"

"Kinesha's mother, Mrs. Johnson," Toby said.

Beside us, someone said, "Mr. Benton is up next."

Toby grinned. "That's who I'm going to dunk."

We pushed through the crowd to the front. The water tank was old aluminum, pitted everywhere. Four feet deep, about ten feet across. The platform for the dunking victim hung about four feet above the water. To get on it, you climbed five steps at the back of the tank. At the side, the platform connected to a target. A faded target with faded white circles, not even a red bull's eye. Mostly just gray aluminum.

Working the water tank was Mr. Porter, the sixth grade social studies teacher. Under the streetlight, his face was as pitted as the aluminum tank. Even his eyes were gray irises within a faded white circle. I had been at this school for the last four years and I had never seen him smile. Wasn't looking forward to being in his class this year.

One of the dads, a guy with long arms, stepped up to the throwing line. He tossed the ball up and down. Then, almost without looking or aiming, he wound up and threw.

Clang! The ball bounced off the target.

We yelled disappointment, along with everyone else: Mrs. Johnson stayed dry.

She whistled "Amazing Grace," off-tune, like she didn't care if she fell in or not.

Yeah, right. I could see she was holding on tight.

I kept track of the next six throws. Four hit just left of center and two went wild. Would have gone across the street and knocked out a car window, except someone was smart enough to set up a net to catch the balls.

Another dad stepped up. Tipping back his baseball cap, he called, "Ready to get wet?"

"You couldn't hit a barn," Mrs. Johnson hooted back.

This dad was a southpaw, a leftie. He wound up, then whipped his arm around. Clang!

Dead center!

Mrs. Johnson must have felt the mechanism beneath her move: her mouth puckered in surprise—Oh!—then she plummeted—Splash!

Hoots and hollers, everyone cheered.

Mrs. Johnson came up spluttering, but grinning. "Towel. Where's the towel?" She wiped off her shiny brown face and toweled her hair while wading to the stairs in back.

Mr. Porter had reset the platform and now called, "Who's up next?"

Mr. Benton raised both hands, "That's me."

A whoop rose from the kids. A chance to dunk the principal!

Mr. Benton was African-American, tall and dark, with a shaved bald head. Parents liked him all right, and for a principal, he was okay. Tonight, he wore basketball shorts, a school T-shirt and flip-flops, ready to get wet.

While Mr. Benton climbed onto the Victim's Throne, we rushed to line up. I'd been ready for this, and held off younger kids for Toby to get near the front, third in line. Waiting, Toby rocked back and forth again. Nervous.

A little kid, maybe a third grader, was the first to throw. "You're gonna get wet!" he called to Mr. Benton, and his friends all laughed and cheered.

Over the heads of the two in front of us, Mr. Porter spotted me and asked, "So. Is the Bread Project on or off?"

I lifted a shoulder. "Don't know."

"Well, I hope that project is off," Mr. Porter said. "Everyone baking bread as a fund raiser? I told Griff last spring, when he first started talking about it, it won't work."

At last, someone who was against the Bread Project. But not someone who was likely to help. Embarrassed, I concentrated on Mr. Benton, who was kicking his long legs in the water.

"There you are, Toby. Are you about to throw?" Mrs. Zane suddenly appeared. She still had Veronica on her hip, and the smaller boys trailed after her. Her eyes widened. "Oh, Mr. Benton is on the dunking seat. What fun! Look, boys!"

The blond boys squirmed past me and into the front of the crowd, pushing against the short fence that held everyone back.

"Mr. Porter. So nice to see you." Mrs. Zane reached past me to shake Mr. Porter's hand, then said, "How's the new foster girl working out? What's her name?"

Foster girl? Mr. Porter and his sister? I groaned in disgust. My days in foster care were long gone, but I would never forget how bad they were.

"Her name is Alli Flynn."

"Where is she tonight?"

Mr. Porter pointed behind us.

Startled, I spun around: Alli was two people back. I thought she had stayed inside, but here she was. I hadn't known she was living with Mr. Porter. Poor kid. He would be one of the worst foster parents. Always thinking how he was doing her a big favor.

Mrs. Zane called, "Hello, Alli. Going to throw?"

Alli nodded back.

Mrs. Zane said, "Mr. Porter, it was so thoughtful of you to bring her to the party. She needs to meet people, and you're already doing a great job with her."

"Thank you." Mr. Porter shrugged, his thin shoulders jerking up, then down. "It's my first time, but I'll do my best."

I ground my teeth and thought of Alli as I'd first seen her, abandoned in the gym. Would I be in her shoes soon? Never.

Looking at Toby and me, Mr. Porter said, "Are you going to throw balls or just stand there?"

Startled that we were up already, I dug into my jean pocket and pulled out my last dollar. The paper was limp from the folding and re-folding. I exchanged it for three baseballs.

"Ready?" I asked Toby, and he nodded.

The target seemed to be right on: hit it square in the center, and the person would drop.

"OK, the target is a bit off," I said. "Pull to the left and you'll drop him."

Toby glanced at me and tightened his jaw. Then he focused on the gray and white circles.

His brothers started a chant, "Drop him! Drop him! Drop him!" And the crowd took it up.

Toby made a show of winding up. He flung the ball. Clang!

It hit the faded white line just left of the bull's eye. Nothing. Mr. Benton was still smiling.

I shook my head and kept my face straight. "What a shame. Try just north of center. Or just south. Gotta be a sweet spot somewhere."

Toby didn't look at me, he just concentrated. His next two pitches went fast. Clang! Clang!

"No!" Toby slapped his hands together. "Too bad!" He pulled a dollar from his pocket. "Here, let me have three more balls."

Mrs. Zane was there, though, saying, "No, honey. It's time to go inside."

"Mom! I know I can drop him. Let me try! Just one more!"

She put her arm around his shoulder and pulled Toby out of the line and off to the side, while the rest of the Zanes and I followed. My stomach started cramping, not from hunger, but from hurting for Toby's pride. Toby could have dropped Mr. Benton, and man, that would have been great to watch.

"Down, Mommy. Put me down," Veronica whined.

The crowd quieted while the next person got ready to throw. Clang!

"Toby, your Dad gives a speech in ten minutes. Come in and listen."

Clang!

"Do I have to?" He frowned and shot me a glare. "Can't I throw just one more time?"

Clang! A roar of disappointment. Mr. Benton was still dry.

"Yes, you have to come inside. No, you can't throw again."

"We'll be right in," I answered for both of us. Otherwise Toby would argue and argue and argue until Mrs. Zane got really mad.

Mrs. Zane nodded at me, gave Toby a "you-better-obey" stare, and led her blond ducklings back into the school building.

Toby didn't let me say anything. He just whipped out his billfold and peeled off five-dollar bills. "Five, ten, fifteen, twenty, twenty-five." Then he peeled off a couple more. "Oh, here, take ten more, just for the heck of it. Then we won't have to bet again for a while."

"No, I don't want your money." I folded my arms and tried to swallow. I still had some pride, too. "And we never have to bet again."

Toby stuffed the money in his pocket and stared at the water tank.

I stood numb, unable to say any more. It wasn't like it hurt him to make bets and let me win; his billfold was still stuffed. As Mr. Zane was fond of telling anyone and everyone who would listen, he was a landlord, owning lots of apartment complexes in this neighborhood. He went into a run-down place, bought it, cleaned it up, put in security fences and cameras, and then made sure each renter had a good record. No shady characters in his apartments, he always bragged. Nice and clean apartments like that, they get a good reputation. Long waiting lists.

Last year, I kept expecting the Zanes to move away to a richer, newer part of town. But then Mr. Zane got elected councilman: he has to stay in this voting district. Toby would be my friend for at least four more years.

Finally, Toby sighed and pulled out the bills again. "Look, a bet's a bet."

"Only twenty-five," I said stiffly. "Only what we bet."

Toby's mouth was straight and tight. But he counted out the twenty-five.

With trembling hands, I took the money. Now I wouldn't have to bother Marj. Would she ever remember that I needed an allowance? Because I sure wasn't going to ask. And I sure wasn't going to bet with Toby again. It wasn't worth ruining a friendship.

Clang!

Alli was throwing. Her arms were so scrawny that I didn't think she could even throw a tennis ball, much less a baseball.

Toby said, "Bet the sweet spot is the very center. Bet I could hit it."

Alli wound up and threw. Not hard, but not soft. And—by luck—it hit smack in the target's center.

Mr. Benton squealed like a second-grader. Plop! Splash!

A tremendous wave rolled toward the edge of the water tank; it rolled toward Mr. Porter, still high, still strong, it splashed over the edge, right onto Mr. Porter's chest; water ran down his pant legs.

Alli stood stock still, eyes wide, shocked, her pale face even paler. Mrs. Johnson–now in dry clothes–leapt up and down shouting and clapping. Mr. Benton rose up, flinging his head back, spraying water everywhere and roaring with laughter. And kids were laughing and pointing at the new girl, who had dunked the principal.

And Toby whispered, "I could have dropped him."

With Mr. Benton's dunking, they shut down the water tank. "The rest of the activities will be inside," Mr. Porter called.

We waited around, talking to some of the guys, until finally heading in ourselves. Inside, Toby reminded me, "You still need to talk to Mrs. Lopez."

"Right. Save me a place to listen to your Dad."

Toby nodded and headed toward the row of chairs.

Of course, I heard Mrs. Lopez before I saw her. She and Marj sat at the PTA table near the gym door. Coming from the side, I saw the stacks of paper money and coins that, apparently, they had just counted. Marj was writing something on a pad of paper.

Mr. Benton was there, too, already dried off from the water tank, and wearing a school T-shirt.

This was bad: with all three of them together, they had to be discussing the Bread Project. I didn't mean to eavesdrop, but they were loud.

Pointing to the cash, Mrs. Lopez said, "We've enough to pay the bill for the T-shirts. From now on, it's just profit. But we need another fundraiser. We all understand the idea of the Bread Project, but we need to decide: do this project or something else."

Marj had a hand to her ear, playing with her dangly earring, a bad habit. "Will it work? I've never done anything like this."

Mr. Benton nodded, while Mrs. Lopez said, "*Si*, it will work."

No, I thought, it won't, and then I sped up, darting around the last few people, but bumping against a PTA table. I'd have to go around it to join the conversation.

Marj said, "Okay. But I'd feel better if we worked out all the details first."

Mrs. Lopez shook her head. "There's no time to work everything out. Besides, we don't have enough sourdough starter to give each student. The only way to get enough is to let it grow week by week. Which means we must start now, or wait until next year."

"You're right. It will be a couple weeks anyway before very many kids get the starter. We can easily work out details as we go, but we have to start now," Mr. Benton said. "It's agreed then? The Bread Project is on?"

Rage shot through me and my fists clenched as I hurried around the table.

How to explain? Griff's ideas about fund-raising for the school had a history; they were tied to who he was, a symbol of everything he stood for. It wasn't a plan for anyone to just pick up and use. Without Griff, there was nothing.

Marj saw me and nodded me over. "Oh. Here's Eliot. Griff's son. Eliot." She cleared her throat. "Our son." She coughed. "As a family, we appreciate you doing this to honor Griff. He would be happy about this."

Son.

Earlier, I had longed for Marj to call me her son. Now? I don't know what she meant. She said it so awkwardly, like she didn't know if she meant it. Said, "our son," not "my son."

Mr. Benton asked me, "You okay with this Bread Project?"

Son. Marj had called me son. Had said we were a family. I couldn't speak, the heavy misery holding me in its tight fist.

Mr. Benton slapped my back. The guys' version of Mrs. Lopez's hug of sympathy.

Still, I said nothing, held fast by the weight of grief.

"Oh," Marj said to me, "Here's a T-shirt for you."

It was a size large. Too big for me.

"Good," Mr. Benton said. "We'll get the Project started tomorrow."

When I slid into the metal chair beside Toby, he whispered, "Well?"

"Too late. The Project is on." I didn't know what to think about it, whether I should be mad or not. It had all seemed so easy before Marj had called me "our son." I did know one thing: I would not get involved with the Bread Project. Not at all.

In front of us, Mr. Zane was talking into a microphone and gesturing. Sameer, sitting with his mother on the front row, was hanging over the back of his chair and watching a kid behind him play with a hand-held video game. The family with dark-haired twin boys sat outside of the row of chairs and let the boys wrestle on the floor. Toward the back were two rows of Arab-looking men and women with head-scarves, the Herat clan.

The microphone squealed and someone behind us said, "Zany Zanes."

Toby hitched his chair closer, leaned over and whispered, "The Bread Project is so complicated. I bet–"

Surprised, I leaned back and studied Toby's face: he was going to bet something again? He had straight white-blond hair and a long straight nose–if his hair darkened as he grew older, he'd look just like his dad.

"–that the Bread Project will fail." Toby sat back up and stared at his dad.

This bet made me mad. "So, what else is new? Of course it will fail." But Toby wasn't supposed to think that, much less say it.

He leaned back in: "What's new is my twenty-five dollars to back up the bet. Just a bet between friends."

I sucked in breath. I thought we weren't betting any more. Was he trying to say that he was okay with what happened earlier, okay with not getting to dunk Mr. Benton?

"In fact, it will fail so badly that I'll double that bet," he said.

"Done." I couldn't pass up that kind of money. Automatically, I announced the exact terms of the bet. "The bet isn't finished until Thanksgiving, when we either have 500 loaves or we don't. If the Bread Project works, then I win."

"Agreed."

And I thought: I might make it through school this year with friends like Toby.

Later, back in my room, I laid out my clothes, supplies and backpack, trying to be organized for the first day of school. If only emotions could be lined up so easily. Downstairs, I knew Marj was putting together a computer presentation for tomorrow. She only had a couple slides done, so she'd be up late. But she wouldn't let me help, just told me to go up and get ready for bed.

With everything ready, I flopped onto my bed and stared at a framed picture of Griff and me, holding up a catfish we had caught together. What a great morning that had been: seven catfish in just two hours. That night, we had a fish fry with Mr. and Mrs. James, the old couple down the street who talked with a Southern drawl. That was Griff. Always bringing in someone that others had overlooked. It had been a day of sun and laughter and good food and good friends.

Suddenly, I flipped the picture face down, jumped off the bed, jerked the curtains closed, took off my shoes, threw my T-shirt into the dirty clothesbasket, and plopped back onto the bed. Trying not to think. Oh. How I missed Griff.

And how hard it was with Marj. Did I think of her as just an almost-adoptive mother or as a real mother? Had she meant what she said, that we were a family? Did she really think of me as a son? Her son?

BREAD PROJECT: DAY 1

ELIOT

I slouched into my seat, smack in the front-center of the auditorium. In the middle of all the kindergartners and first graders. Toby and the rest of the sixth grade sat on the back row, but I had to run the computer for Marj's presentation on the screen up front.

A kid poked my back. I jerked around, hitting my elbow on the wooden armrest. I gasped and shifted in the hard seat to glare at the kids behind me. "What?"

"Why are we here?" asked a girl with a high-pitch voice.

"It's an assembly."

Her eyes were wide. "What's that?"

Kindergartners. I shook my head. They didn't know anything about anything yet. "Just watch," I said.

The house lights darkened. Bright stage lights washed out the red velvet curtains. Swish, the curtains opened.

"Oh! Look!" The little kids squealed and jabbed fingers, pointing.

For a change, they were right; it was a wonder. I sat forward. All along the edge of the stage, almost on top of blue or red floor lights, marched quart jars. They didn't gleam or twinkle. Instead, they glowed. 'Course it was a glow borrowed from the lights, but still a sight to see.

Then I saw a splash of white hit one of the jars. A spitball.

No! They couldn't do that to the bread jars. I half rose–then stopped.

Careful, I told myself. Don't get involved in the Bread Project, I reminded myself. Even this computer thing, it was just to help Marj, not the Project.

I dropped back into my seat. And it squeaked.

And I remembered what Griff always said: when you're about to do something crazy, try to distract yourself. Maybe I could distract the others and still stay out of it.

With both hands, I grabbed my seat's edge and rocked. There. Now that was a satisfying, annoying creaky rhythm. "Hey, kids. Listen."

"Huh?'

"Listen," I whispered loudly. Creak-a-creak-creak.

"Like this?" It was the girl with the high voice. Her seat squeaked better than mine. I smiled at her, then grinned, as the creak spread in arcs through the kids seated behind her.

It worked. More and more seats took up the joy of creaking until I was sure no one was interested in throwing spitballs at the bread jars. And such a great sound.

Mr. Benton strode across the stage and behind him was Marj. Into the microphone, Mr. Benton said, "Welcome to the first assembly of the year."

I didn't listen to his introduction. I just stared at the 512 quart jars which I had just saved from a spit ball war. They were the beginning of the Bread Project.

❖

"Good morning," Marj said into the microphone. "This assembly is the kick-off for the First Annual Bread Project, a community project that was planned by my late husband, Griff Winston."

The projector's fan blew warm air at me, and I shifted in my seat to avoid it. The first time Griff brought Marj to meet me, on that hopeful day last year, her voice had been warm. Like milk chocolate was melting in her mouth. Today, talking about the Bread Project, it had changed. It was deeper, fuller, like she had been eating dark chocolate. Last night, she had been scared to meet people, yet here she was talking to the auditorium full of kids. It had been a huge, slow effort last night to put together this presentation; she had stayed up until 1 or 2 a.m. But the presentation would keep her on track, make sure she didn't get too emotional.

Mr. Benton walked off the side of the stage, leaving Marj alone.

I held the remote control tightly, making sure I was ready.

"Today," Marj said, "one person will take home one of these quart jars with sourdough starter." She didn't use her hands to explain things like Griff had always done; instead, she raised an eyebrow, or frowned, or smiled. Now, she smiled, as if to say, "I know this Bread Project sounds strange, but give me a minute and I'll explain."

I started the first slide showing an empty quart jar, a quart jar with sourdough starter, and a loaf of bread.

Marj continued: "Sourdough starter is just wild yeast. Yeast is the stuff that helps make bread rise and be light and fluffy. Without it, bread would be as hard as a rock."

Next slide: flat bread and bread that had risen.

"This particular sourdough starter has been in the Winston family for over a hundred and fifty years." The next slide showed an old black and white picture of Griff's family, including his aunt wearing an apron and holding out a loaf of bread.

I knew most kids wouldn't understand the importance of that. Yeast– if they ever thought about it at all–was just stuff that came out of a package. But a yeast culture could live for years and years. Griff had been proud of the 150-year-old starter. "One of the oldest cultures in the United States," he said.

Marj continued, explaining that each jar with its starter would come with instructions (click to next slide) and recipes (click to next slide). The starter had to be fed with flour and water each week (click to next slide), which would let the yeast grow.

So far, I thought Marj was doing great. The Kindergartners were quiet and the only sound was a few chairs creaking. But Marj better hurry, 'cause the kids would get restless fast. For the next set of slides, I anticipated when she would get there and clicked early. It worked, speeding her up.

"Next week, the first person will pass one cup of starter on to the next person. Then two people will have the sourdough starter. They will feed it and let it grow a week and then, the next week, those two will give to two more, so there will be four jars of starter. Double that the next week for eight jars of starter."

My slides flickered–quickly–on the cracked screen behind Marj. Quickly. Explaining how each week the number of jars of sourdough starter would double. By Thanksgiving, ten weeks from now–1, 2, 4, 8, 16, 32, 64, 128, 256, 512–there would be 512 jars. Enough for each student to take home a jar of starter.

The kindergarten kid on my left side was kicking his legs, and the girl on my right had pulled her legs up to sit cross-legged. She studied a scab on her knee, and then leaned close and whispered, "What's a Ress-uh-Pee?"

I rolled my eyes and hoped the older kids understood better. For these little kids, Mrs. Lopez and the PTA had better send letters to the parents.

"On Sunday of Thanksgiving week," Marj said, "you'll start your bread. You can make anything you want with the sourdough, any recipe you want. Sometime on Monday night, you'll bake that bread. On Tuesday, the last day of school before Thanksgiving break, you'll bring your loaf of bread to school for the PTA Thanksgiving Dinner. We'll eat a turkey dinner (click: slide of a party, with a big turkey on a platter) and then auction (click: slide of an auctioneer banging down a gavel. Sold!) the bread as a fundraiser. The PTA will use the money to buy playground equipment."

Marj's eyes widened and she smiled, obviously expecting the audience to do something. Clap or cheer, maybe?

Creak-a-creak creak. The little kids were at it again. Annoying, but better than spitballs on the glass jars.

Marj frowned. She spoke louder, like louder would make it easier to understand. "We'll sell the bread. With that money, we'll buy monkey bars. Swings. Slides and tunnels. Would you like a new playground?"

Silence.

"Hurrah!" I called weakly.

Marj waved her hands overhead: "A new playground! Hurrah!"

Behind me, another kid yelled, "Hurrah!"

"Let's all cheer for a new playground. Ready?" Marj raised her arm, and then dropped it. "Hurrah!"

A weak cheer dribbled from the crowd.

"One more time!"

"Hurrah!" Louder, this time. The kids sensed a reason to pay attention again: a chance to make noise.

"Hurrah!" Marj called.

"Hurrah!" Finally, the sound was louder. Still not enthusiastic. Still not real cheering. But noise, anyway.

While they yelled and called, I thought about the Project. Griff had worried about it, because this was a Pyramid Scheme.

The Internet explained a Pyramid Scheme just like Marj had described. One person passes on something to a second. Those two pass on to two more, which makes four; those four pass on to four more, which makes eight; and so on, until you get the 512 people participating. Mostly, the Pyramid Scheme was used by shady salesmen. When it worked, it could make lots of money. But it almost always failed. 'Cause somewhere, someone would fail to pass it on, or fail to sell it to the next person.

Say, for example, that on the fourth week, half the eight kids didn't bring the sourdough starter to pass on. Then, instead of having 512 loaves at ten weeks, there would only be 256. On any given week, if even one kid forgot to bring the sourdough starter, it would mess up the final count.

And then there's the question of who would buy the bread at an auction. Griff said, "It's like an old-fashioned pie supper. Wives will ask their husbands to buy their bread. Friends will buy friend's bread. It's a community thing."

Yes, the Bread Project was a failure just waiting to happen.

Well, at least Marj had made it through the assembly without any major problems. Just a few more minutes and we'd be done.

Mr. Benton was back on stage now, trying to quiet the kids. "Time to listen." After several tries, the noise went back to a slight creak-a-creak.

He held out a paper bag, "This bag has the names of all the sixth graders, and we'll start there. The lower grades will get their sourdough starter just a few weeks before Thanksgiving."

Marj reached in and pulled out a folded yellow slip of paper. She shook it open. She smoothed it out on the podium. She looked at the paper, looked up at the students, looked down, then up again. "Okay. The first person to receive the sourdough starter is an important person."

I held my breath. I had tried to get Marj to pick Toby first. Mrs. Zane would make sure the project got off to a good start. But Marj had insisted on the luck of the draw.

Marj cleared her throat. "I need this student to come up to the stage. Alli Flynn."

Oh, no. Porter's foster kid. Could it get any worse?

ALLI

Sitting there in the auditorium, I yawned. Sleeping at Mr. Porter's was bad. Stiff bed, scratchy blankets. Mostly, I lay there last night looking at the patterns on the ceiling from the streetlights. Wondering when Ted would let me come home.

The wooden auditorium chairs weren't comfortable, either, but I let my eyes close. Resting. Daydreaming. This whole Bread Project thing, it sounded like a disaster. Even I knew that every week some kid would forget to bring back their jar.

1-2-4-8-16-32-64. It would be the sixth or seventh week before anyone outside sixth grade would get the starter. The last three or four weeks, there would finally be enough jars of starter for the lower grades.

Idly, I wondered how many jars there would be if you kept going until New Year's, just five weeks later? Bet we would have to do a similar math problem in some class.

"–Alli Flynn."

Startled, I sat up. Looked around. Elbowed the girl on my right. "What do they want with Alli Flynn?"

She squinted and stared at my throat, obviously surprised by my rough voice. "That girl is supposed to go up on stage."

"Why?"

"She gets the first jar of sourdough starter."

"Oh." I was stunned. Me?

Mr. Benton said my name again. "Alli Flynn. Come up, please."

He wanted me up there on stage. In front of all these eyes. I was okay talking to people one at a time. But crowds? That was different.

But I had no choice.

The girl shrank back, so I could get out to the aisle. Nervous, I stuck my hands in my pockets and let my hair swing down to hide my face. I was too skinny, and this second-hand plaid uniform was so baggy and so long. Miss Porter hadn't had time to fit it or hem it.

Crowds. Too many nameless people. I couldn't tell what they were thinking, hated not knowing the people who looked at me. Wanted to say: Stop staring third-grade-girl with the huge bow in your hair because I don't even know your name.

While I walked forward, Mr. Benton came down the steps heading for the fourth grade section. Some kid over there was wailing.

At last, I reached the stairs. The wooden steps sagged, creaked. And the last step was only half the height of the others. How old was this school building anyway?

And then I was on stage.

Appropriate (Latin derivation: a-p-p-r-o-p-r-i-a-t-e.) For the last week, I'd felt like an actress. The real Alli Flynn was back in her familiar bedroom, getting ready to start sixth grade with her friends, practicing spelling bee words with Ted. This Alli Flynn was pure actress, nothing about her was real.

"Alli Flynn, you'll be the first person to take home a jar of sourdough starter." Mrs. Winston held out a jar that was half full of a white liquid. "Will you promise to follow these directions carefully? And next Friday, will you bring back a cup of starter to pass on to the next person?"

"Yes, ma'am." My voice quivered, and I could barely hear myself. Oh, bad acting, I thought.

"Speak up." Mrs. Winston gave me a small smile of encouragement. "You're sure. You'll bring it back next week?"

I leaned into the microphone and said loudly, dramatically, "Why, yes, ma'am, I promise."

At that, Mrs. Winston's eyebrows went up, and I thought she might smile at me. But she just whispered that I could go and sit down now. I clutched the jar to my chest. I slid my feet along, shuffling, trying not to echo as I crossed the stage. Careful of the odd-height step, I stopped at the top. When I started down, though, my heel caught on the hem of my too-long uniform.

I lurched forward. Then jerked back, losing my balance. Heart thumping, arms waving.

Oh! The bread jar flew upward. Kindergartners gasped. I reached for the jar, then fought to keep my balance and not fall off the steps. There! I touched the jar, palms flat. It steadied in my hand. But stretching, reaching, my balance tipped again. And so did the jar.

It was like bad juggling: the jar bobbled up, then down, glittering in the stage lights.

I saw that boy, Eliot, diving over little kids, stretched out, reaching.

Then it hit; the jar hit the auditorium floor and shattered. Sprayed the front row with sourdough starter. I barely saw that just before I landed, sprawling down three steps headfirst.

"Oh! Oh! Oh!" Mrs. Winston wailed into the microphone.

I sagged, afraid I was hurt bad. But I didn't feel pain anywhere, so I pushed up and tried to sit on a step.

For a long minute, my eyes registered the activity around me, but I felt nothing: A dark-haired kindergarten boy jumped around and slapped at the sourdough on his shirt, screaming. Eliot was suddenly there, holding the kid, keeping him from hurting himself. A teacher pointed at me, and I looked down. My right knee bled, a scrape or a cut. Three other teachers corralled the whining kids, keeping them away from broken glass. A teacher from the back of the room–she had short, spiky hair–sprinted down the aisle, calling for the janitor. Finally, Mr. Benton pushed aside some jars, put a hand on the edge of the stage and jumped up. Took the microphone away from Mrs. Winston, who was still wailing.

With a quiet voice, he took control, organizing teachers and calming students.

I looked down at the broken glass. At the splatter of thin dough. My face moved, tried to smile at how ironic this was. It wasn't the way they wanted, but the Bread Project was already spreading.

A man with a bushy mustache, the janitor I guessed, pushed a yellow mop bucket in front of him and trundled down the center aisle and started cleaning up the glass and the mess. Six or seven younger kids marched away to wash sourdough starter off their clothes. Some were probably going to the nurse's office, too, for Band-Aids. I was still frozen, stunned at the chaos.

Mrs. Winston came beside me, gently offering me a hand and pulling me up. She smiled and nodded and murmured, "That's a shame."

At her kindness, tears filled my eyes. I had ruined everything; it was my fault. Just like with Mandy. Six weeks ago, Mandy and I were getting ready to go to the swimming pool. I was chattering on Mandy's cell phone to a friend, and I tossed my hot pink beach towel over my shoulder.

"Don't drag your towel on the ground," Mandy said automatically.

I didn't even hear her. Or didn't listen. Only later, when I replayed the scene in my mind did I remember those words. At the time, though, I just dashed down the steps toward the car.

Except Mandy was following right behind me and stepped on the towel.

It was my fault.

She fell down the steps and lay there in her black swim suit, with the edge of the pink towel still under the flip-flops on her feet, and she was holding the ball of her stomach, moaning, and it was my fault, and we still don't know if the baby will be okay or not.

I did the right things after that. I called 911–the cell phone was in my hands. I called Ted. I sat quiet at the hospital. I sat quiet in the car. I sat quiet all that night. The doctor said the baby–a girl, it was a girl!–seemed to be okay for now, but they would have to wait a couple weeks to know for sure.

I helped with the cooking and cleaning that next week, until Mandy's mom came. I did things right.

But it was my fault. Then and now.

"I'm sorry, I didn't mean to do it." I tried to stand and rush down the steps and hide in the crowd. But Mrs. Winston used her thumbs to wipe away my tears. She didn't see that my knee was bleeding. She just murmured, "You okay?"

At my nod, she pulled me up and kept hold of my hand and pulled me back to the microphone. Mr. Benton stepped aside and let Mrs. Winston take the mike. She looked around at the audience and cleared her throat.

The room quieted. Except for the kindergartners at the front squeaking their chairs.

I stood there, miserable. Looking down at my shoes. Would they send me to a different school?

Mrs. Winston laid a hand on my shoulder and spoke to the crowd. "This was just an accident, an unfortunate accident."

I was ready to apologize, but–I didn't understand–she wasn't giving me the microphone, wasn't letting me say, I'm sorry.

She cleared her throat. "It's always difficult when you plan something and then it starts with an accident. But this time, it's easy to fix. This evening, I'll make sure Alli Flynn gets another jar of starter."

Wait. I looked up at her face. She was giving me another jar of starter? After that mess? She was giving me another chance?

The auditorium was silent.

"New playground equipment!" Mrs. Winston was fake-cheerful. "Monkey bars and swings! Slides and tunnels!"

Silence.

Mrs. Winston glanced over at me, then suddenly bent to look at my knee. "Oh, let's get you to the school nurse."

Mr. Benton took over the microphone again while Mrs. Winston held my arm and hustled me down the steps and up the aisle and through the maze of hallways to the nurse's office. All the while, I marveled: She didn't blame me. Just an accident, she said.

At that moment, I would have done anything for Mrs. Winston.

ELIOT

Off and on the rest of the day, I watched that girl, Alli Flynn. She was like a sleepwalker. In Mr. Crum's pre-algebra class, she ignored everything that was happening. Once, Mr. Crum called on her, but she just yawned and said, "I don't know."

I flinched at her voice. At the party the night before, she had barely said five words, but even then I noticed her rough voice. It was like a washing machine that was off balance, sort of liquidy and thumpy and harsh at the same time.

I didn't want to listen to that voice.

But I had to talk to her about the Bread Project and get her straightened out. How do you talk to a girl, though, without getting teased?

The bell rang and I escaped Crum's class and raced to World History, and I didn't see Alli again until after lunch when I raced into Physical Science just under the bell and stopped cold.

What was that smell? I pinched my nose and whirled to the teacher, "Sulfur?"

Miss Garrett had short, spiky hair and wore khaki trousers, but still looked more dressed up than the older teachers. They all wore the school T-shirt with faded jeans.

"Yes," she said, "We're doing an experiment today."

Now Miss Garrett's voice, it was like a small, brass bell, full of good cheer.

I stumbled away from the smell, toward the back. But the only open seat was behind Alli. She was in the front seat, the row beside the door, up against the wall. Maybe I'd get a chance during class to talk to her.

"Hey," Alli said, as I passed her, "Watch it!"

I hadn't meant to hit her with my backpack, but she'd never believe that. I slouched into the seat and let my backpack plunk onto the floor. As expected, Alli glared at me. Irritating voice, irritating girl.

I liked listening to Miss Garret's bell-voice. She told us about going to college and why she loved science, using the words, "gung-ho" about five times. Then she talked about where she had traveled that summer and how she had just gotten engaged. "We'll get married at Christmas, so I won't miss any days with you. In January, my new name will be Mrs. Shane Baxter."

I turned ninety degrees, putting my back to the wall and sticking my knees into the aisle, so I could see the rest of the class. The girls had sloppy smiles at the news of a romance. The guys were looking out the window or at something on their desks. Me, I was happy that all this chatter kept us from doing that demo lab with sulfur. Maybe she would be easy to get off topic all the time, and we wouldn't have to work very hard in science this year.

Finally, Miss Garrett called roll and made each person stand and tell one scientific fact they found hard to believe. "It will help me get to know each of you better," she said.

We groaned, but Miss Garrett insisted.

Marissa Blue said, "I can't believe men really walked on the moon."

That was good for a five-minute off-the-topic conversation. But finally, Miss Garrett moved on.

Alli stood up and smoothed down her uniform. Too bad she couldn't smooth out her rough voice. "I can't believe," she croaked, "that a person's hand has 1500 bacteria on every square centimeter. I read that in the newspaper this morning."

I shivered. And remembered. Each of my hands carried millions of bacteria. Millions.

Actually–billions.

It had been three years since I'd felt like this.

I wiped my hands down my pants. That made them feel even dirtier. I shivered again, harder this time, until I had to clench my fists to make them stop shaking. I closed my eyes and took deep breaths. I hadn't taken meds for panic for over a year now. Was it coming back?

Miss Garrett suddenly said, "Alli, is your knee bleeding?"

I opened my eyes. Alli was bent over looking at the knee that had been cut that morning. Blood had soaked through the bandage.

"Go the nurse's office and ask her to change that." Miss Garrett held out a hall pass.

"Don't know how to get there," Alli said. "It's my first week."

"Oh, you're new this year." Miss Garrett looked at me. "What's your name?"

"Eliot Winston."

"You know where the nurse's office is?"

Around us, the room went suddenly still. Miss Garrett's head came up, and she scanned the room to see what was wrong. She had no idea.

Brad Garcia, from the back of the room, said, "Miss Garrett, you're new here, so you don't know–"

But I cut him off. "It's okay. I have to go there sometime. It's okay."

And before anyone else could speak, I stood, took the hall pass from Miss Garrett's hand and stalked out, not looking back to see if Alli was following or not, walking numbly toward the school nurse's office, like I'd done a jillion times in the last four years at this school. Only difference? Griff, my Dad, he wouldn't be there.

Alli jogged a couple steps to catch up with me, then matched my pace. "So glad to be out of there," she said. "That smell. Awful! You think science will smell that bad every day?"

"Your knee isn't bothering you much," I muttered.

"Nope. Wasn't complaining. But a good excuse to get out of there."

"Yeah."

"Hey, I'm excited about the Bread Project. That lady, she's your mom, right? She was real nice to me. I'll try to do everything right."

"What?" I needed my privacy. Never mind that bet with Toby. I needed this girl to be unreliable, to let the Bread Project die a natural death. Instead, she sounded very sincere. I had to convince her to kill off the sourdough starter and never pass it on.

But we were already at the doorway of the nurse's office. The new nurse had a long ponytail and looked young like Miss Garrett. A brass sign on her desk read, "Miss Clay, N.C.S.N."

"Can I help you?" she said.

Alli pointed at her knee. "I need a clean Band-Aid."

"Ah, the Bread Project girl," Miss Clay said. "Sit there and I'll get a clean Band-Aid." Miss Clay's voice was soothing, like running a hand over suede. Nothing at all like Alli's voice.

While Miss Clay opened a cabinet and pulled out supplies, I looked around.

The office had been repainted. No more institutional green, but sky blue. Diplomas hung behind the desk, with photos on the desk and bookshelf. A plush navy rug covered the worn spots on the floor.

I had made one of those worn spots, Griff always teased me. Probably true. I had rolled my chair back and forth, back and forth, from Griff's desk to the other desk. Hundreds of times. For the last two years, I had done my homework here, in this room.

The chairs looked fancy now, with blue plaid pillows. Griff would have laughed at that.

"Finished inspecting my office?" Miss Clay stared at me. "What are you looking for anyway?"

"Nothing." And a wave of relief washed over me. It wasn't Griff's room any longer. The new paint, the rug, the pictures–Griff's office would never be so, well, so girly.

I took a deep breath. Still smelled of alcohol and Pine-Sol. But every school nurse's office smelled that way. I met Miss Clay's gaze and smiled. "Just looking around."

She had a hand on her hip, watching me. "You can go on back to class."

But Alli said, "It's my first week, I'll get lost."

Miss Clay nodded that it was okay for me to stay, then turned to the supply cabinet.

The intercom buzzed. "Miss Clay, phone call," said the school secretary's voice. Talk about voices. Mrs. Epstein's voice was a grandmother's voice, old and cracked, like a chipped china tea cup that had seen better days.

Miss Clay buzzed back, "Who is it?"

"Some gentleman. Says he needs to talk to you. Right away."

"Okay, I'll be right there." She said to Alli. "You don't mind waiting a minute, do you? I do real estate sales on weekends, and I've been waiting for a house buyer to call. I'll explain that I'm busy and call back later."

Alli smiled. "Miss Garrett is doing an experiment with sulfur. It stinks."

"I know, I've smelled it all the way down here." Miss Clay shook her head, then stepped into the hallway.

"Oh." It was my chance to get Alli straightened out about the Bread Project. But it was hard to talk about Marj and Griff and everything. I needed a diversion.

ALLI

I pulled off the old Band-Aid and studied the cut on my knee. Should heal easily. Just needed to quit bleeding. I grabbed a gauze pad from Miss Clay's desk and held it to the cut.

Meanwhile, Eliot sat in Miss Clay's chair and pulled open the bottom drawer.

"Hey, what are you doing?"

He didn't answer, just pulled the drawer out more. Till it barely hung in the desk. Reached in the back and pulled out a pack of playing cards. "Entertainment," he said. White stretchy gauze held the cards together.

"How'd you know that was there?" I asked.

Eliot just pulled off the gauze and started shuffling. "Want to play?"

I shrugged. "What game?"

"Rummy."

I tried not to look like the cat that had caught the mouse. "I know that one." How good was Eliot at the game? I threw away the bloody gauze. Miss Clay had a couple dozen Band-Aids laid out, so I picked one and put it on my knee.

Eliot shuffled, dealt. "Um, about the Bread Project."

I scooped up my cards and sorted. "Don't worry. I'll take care of the sourdough starter."

Eliot slapped his cards onto the table and almost exploded, "No."

I pulled my cards against my chest and stared.

"No," he repeated, a little quieter. He picked up the cards and sorted, not looking up while he talked, "It's a crazy project. Won't work. You might as well stop it before it starts."

I folded my cards and crossed my arms. "Why?"

Emotions crossed Eliot's face. Maybe anger. Frustration, for sure. He clenched his jaw and swallowed. "I just don't want the Bread Project to work."

"Great explanation," I said.

"It's none of your business," he said, then tried to distract me by drawing a card and discarding.

I grabbed the discarded card, a Jack of hearts. Tossed out the King of spades. Right away, in the cards I was dealt, I had two sets, 7s and 6s. Should probably lay them down. But I loved to lay down every card at once. Sometimes I got caught with a handful, but still took the chance, hoping for a surprise win.

Eliot frowned at his cards, and then drew one from the deck. Discarded a Jack of diamonds.

With a tight smile, I picked it up and laid down all my cards into neat sets, Jacks, 7s, 6s and I discarded a 10 of clubs. "Gin. Next time we'll have to bet on it. Now, explain about this Bread Project."

"You cheated," he accused.

"Prove it." I was too fast, too smooth. No way had he caught me.

Now he crossed his arms.

"Okay, don't explain the Bread Project," I said.

He said nothing. Just gathered the cards and shuffled.

"The project might fail," I said, "but not 'cause of me. Mrs. Winston is counting on me."

I needed the project to work: Mandy's fall was my fault, but this was a chance to make up for a mistake, the way I could never make it up to Mandy. I was behind this project, and Eliot wouldn't be able to stop me.

Eliot dealt the cards, then picked up his cards one at a time and arranged them. "You're weird."

At my frown, he tried again. "Not bad weird, just weird like me. I like to hold my cards and lay down everything at once, too."

Was he trying to apologize for yelling about the Bread Project? He was the weird one.

"You don't have to answer, but, why are you in the system?" he asked.

"You want the summary? Okay. My mom married a soldier. He went overseas. I was born. My mom died when I was born. I lived with my Grandma. Moved around a lot. Grandma died. State tried to find my dad. He was supposed to be out of the Army by then. Couldn't find him. That's it." I'd said all this so many times that it came out staccato, an audio file playing in an endless loop. It was usually better to lay it all out bluntly, so people would leave me alone about it. "Now, let's play cards."

Eliot didn't laugh or frown or object, just accepted what I'd said. Oddest response I'd ever had. Just accepted all of it. Didn't argue. Didn't try to say, "Poor kid." Which made me study him and wonder about this Bread Project that his mom wanted, but he didn't. What was really going on? I shook my head and sorted my cards. Or, I could be way off base, and he had the best family life ever.

We finished the next hand. Eliot won. 'Course, he cheated. And I let him, watching to see how he'd do it. So I'd know next time. It was in the shuffle, keeping out certain cards. He was fast, I gave him that, but I had seen it happen.

Miss Clay rushed back into the room. "So sorry. It wasn't the buyer, but the realtor, and that realtor always wants to talk and talk."

Eliot shoved the card deck into his pants pocket. How had he known they were in the desk? Why was he taking them?

Miss Clay quickly changed the Band-Aid I had just put on, stopping just long enough to swipe the cut with alcohol and an antibiotic. Then, we had to go back to science.

Walking down the hallway, I said, "You never gave me a good reason to let the Bread Project fail."

Eliot said nothing.

"Okay. When you want to talk, come find me."

ELIOT

That evening, while I waited for Marj to get home, I worked on the website about Griff. I was listening for Marj's car, but I was still surprised when the door from the garage flung open. Clunk!

The doorknob hit the wall. Not good. The doorstop broke last week, and I was supposed to buy a new one today on my way home from school. I slapped my forehead. How did I forget?

I had to get down there right away: I saved and closed my program.

I heard Marj bouncing from wall to wall down the hallway and into the kitchen. Probably too much in her hands. Suddenly, she yelped. Stuff clattered to the floor. "What a full day!"

By the time I got there, it was a mess. Scattered papers. Briefcase fallen over. Shopping bags on top of everything. Marj holding her hip where she must have banged the counter.

I scooped up shopping bags and started putting up groceries while Marj got a glass of water and watched. Couple bananas for Marj and two gallons of milk for me. And a bottle of chocolate syrup to make chocolate milk. She remembered—that made me feel good.

To reach the last bag, I moved the briefcase, uncovering a stack of papers; I wasn't trying to snoop, but the envelope was there, and I was just trying to help. It made my breath catch. A letter from the lawyer, Mr. Donovan. That was his name in the corner of the envelope, wasn't it? It was neatly slit open; Marj had read it. Adoption papers?

I looked up.

Marj saw the letter and frowned. She grabbed the papers and envelopes from my hands, "Here, I'll take those." She snapped up the briefcase, too, and carried everything into her office, right off the living room.

She glanced back and I realized I was staring. Was that letter about the adoption papers? Why was she hiding it? It was yet another question in this long summer of questions.

Mechanically, I jerked up the last plastic bag and pulled out a plastic, wide-mouthed jar. A safety jar for sourdough starter, I guessed. Someone should have thought of using plastic earlier.

Coming back to the kitchen, Marj asked, "Supper ready?"

I tried to remember – that morning – had Marj asked me to cook tonight? "Um, no. I didn't know you wanted me to cook."

"Video games. Right?"

"I didn't have any homework," I said, avoiding her question. I hadn't told her about the website and wouldn't until it was done. She just assumed it was a game. With Griff, now he didn't mind if I played, as long as I had my homework done. But Marj? She hated video games right from the start. I might be off the hook if I told her what I was really doing. But I wasn't ready yet.

Marj just sighed. A deep, tired sigh. She rubbed her eyes and yawned.

"What do we have to cook? You sit and I'll cook fast." I probably sounded as awkward as I felt.

Marj reached down to slip off one brown high heel and then the other. She stood flat-footed and wriggled her toes. "Oh, I don't care. Just do the boxed mac and cheese. I'll just change clothes and be right back to help." She trudged across the living room and disappeared into her bedroom.

I pulled out the pot and started the water boiling, then opened the mac and cheese box. I set the table and poured iced tea–at least I'd made fresh tea when I got home–and set out napkins. By then, my stomach muscles were so tight. I was too anxious to please.

I found a can of peaches and opened that. Marj liked peaches. What else did she like? Salad. The bag of lettuce was already brown, though, and she hadn't bought another. I found a few cherry tomatoes that didn't look too bad. I put three on each plate – she would insist I eat some, too.

Marj reappeared just as the timer on the macaroni went off. She looked more comfortable, at least. Shorts, T-shirt, flip-flops. Her thin legs really did look like toothpicks.

"Feels better just to change clothes," she said and tried to smile.

"Supper's almost ready." I mixed in the cheese powder, milk and butter, and dumped half onto each plate. From a loaf of store-bought bread, I put a slice on each plate.

"Thank, Eliot. I'm just so tired. Thanks." She held up her bread and tried to smile. "Hurrah for bread."

My stomach eased a bit at that, and I picked at my food. Marj shoveled in all of hers, and when I offered, she cleaned off my plate, too. She ate almost all the peaches; I only got one. "I didn't eat lunch," she half-apologized. "But, I did get all my clients' tax statements in on time." She tried to smile again and this time almost made it.

After we ate, Marj cleaned up the kitchen, barely talking. I tried to stay out of her way, but still help, carrying dishes from the table to the sink and throwing away the napkins. Cooking and cleaning the kitchen with Griff, well that had been great, the best part of the day, because he talked and talked and talked. But Marj, now, she was always silent for the first hour after coming home.

"I need to wind down," she explained when she and Griff were dating and she would come over for supper. "Don't tell me anything or ask me anything for an hour, or at least until we've eaten. And cleaned up the kitchen." She had always let Griff do the talking while she walked around like a zombie for an hour.

And it was true, she was more talkative later. Not a lot more talkative, but some. It was just hard for me to wait. Sometimes, I was so full of things to tell someone. Like today, my first day of school. Well, I wouldn't tell her everything today, not anything really about my conversation with Alli about the Bread Project. Well, maybe not much about Miss Clay, either, and how she had redecorated the nurse's office. But Miss Garrett and the sulfur experiment would be interesting to Marj.

So, I sat and waited. Sitting on the bar stool, watching Marj's pale hands dip in and out of the dishwater, watching Marj's freckled face, hoping she would wind down fast.

By the time the last pot was washed and the plates and glasses loaded into the dishwasher, Marj did look more relaxed. "So how was today?" she finally asked. "Did the kids talk about the Bread Project? Are you talking it up?"

Surprised she asked about that first, I said, "Ah, yes. The kids are excited." I paused, feeling awkward again, trying to figure out what to say to please her. But she motioned for me to go on. "You know, some of them, the younger kids especially, they don't understand the Project. But they want a new playground. Yeah. Excited."

Marj's smile–a full smile now, finally–softened her face, and I wanted to make her smile more.

"Griff was so excited about this project," she said. "He talked about it the whole time we were on our honeymoon. Every restaurant, he ordered bread and compared it to his recipes."

"Toby says he's going to find a really good recipe. Something different from everyone else. And a couple kids said their grandmothers made bread from scratch, and they were going to ask for recipes."

"Good, good." Marj opened a cupboard and took out a bag of pretzels and opened them. Seemed like she was always snacking on pretzels at night. At the mall or at a ball game, she loved buying the big soft pretzels covered in kosher salt. Leaning over the kitchen counter, she sighed. Then, she seemed to shake herself and said, "What about the rest of your day?"

While Marj listened and ate pretzels, I talked, thinking I was chattering almost as much as Alli had. After ten minutes or so, she kept asking questions, but she also started working. Set out the new plastic jar and took the sourdough starter from the refrigerator and found the bag of flour and set it beside them. It was simple to feed the starter, hard to mess up, just adding flour and water. That's what made it so easy for Griff's family–my family, the Winston family–to keep it going for over 150 years.

I really played up the story about science class.

"Sulfur! I hate that rotten egg smell," Marj shook her head. "Sounds like a new teacher."

"She is new– "

Ring! Marj found her phone in her purse and flipped it open. "Mrs. Lopez, I'm so glad you called. Just a minute." Marj held her hand over the phone and said, "Go watch TV or something. This might take a minute." She paused, and then said to Eliot, "But we need—"

She hesitated again, but nodded once, like to herself and continued, "—we need to have a serious talk tonight."

"About what?" I asked.

But Marj had already turned away, talking to Mrs. Lopez. It was a long talk about plastic containers for the Bread Project. A fourteen-minute talk. I didn't try to listen, but Marj got loud.

"I didn't know you bought them special," she said. "But there's nothing I can do."

Mrs. Lopez ran a small grocery store and had donated the glass jars, so she'd be really mad that Alli broke the first one. I flipped on the TV, but sat unmoving, letting the images flicker in the darkening living room while I worried: what did Marj want to talk about?

"I'm sorry," Marj said loudly into the phone.

"No, I didn't know you couldn't take them back."

"No. Mr. Benton made the decision. It's for the safety of the children. Glass is just too dangerous."

I closed my eyes. Tried to remember Marj's exact expression when she said we needed to "have a serious talk." Her exact tone of voice.

"I'm sorry." Marj sounded tired now. "You have 500 plastic containers?" She paused. "Yes, I'll bring the glass back tomorrow and pick up the plastic." Pause. "No, it'll have to be after five o'clock, when I'm done at the office."

What had Mr. Donovan, the lawyer, said in that letter? I squirmed. I worried. Was Marj mad at me?

"I'm really sorry." She sounded defensive again.

"I'm really, really sorry."

When she finally hung up, Marj was just as mad, just as tense as she had been before supper.

I decided it was time to take a walk.

I turned off the TV and went to the kitchen. I picked up the plastic container with the sourdough starter. "You're tired. I can walk over to the Porters and take the starter to Alli. Give you a little time to yourself. If you want."

Marj sighed, but shook her head. "No. We need to talk."

ALLI

"I gave you money yesterday," Miss Porter said.

Aggravated, I pulled open the fridge door so I could show her how empty it was.

But her cell phone rang, a ring-tone that meant it was a client. She changed that tone every few weeks, she said, to remind her to keep up with her new clients.

Miss Porter leaned over the kitchen counter. I sighed, and figuring it would be a long conversation, I closed the fridge and settled on a barstool. Waiting.

She talked rapidly about a party at the Country Club tomorrow. She did special events for the club and was coming and going all the time. Didn't have regular office hours. She did parties, weddings, luncheons, anything that someone wanted done, she could make it happen, she bragged. Even her son's golf career: she had gotten him free lessons from the club's pro.

While she talked, Miss Porter shrugged on the navy jacket of her business suit and brushed off the bottoms of her feet before slipping on her heels. "Yes, I can be there in five minutes."

She snapped her cell phone closed and turned to me. Mr. Porter, her brother, had an ugly complexion. Hers? Pink and perfect. They had the same light brown hair, though, and the same gray eyes. "Problems about the food for the McGuire's party. So, I'm off again. Tell my brother not to wait up for me. Where is he anyway?"

"Bowling league."

"Oh. That's why you wanted money. For supper?"

"Yes, ma'am." I had her attention, my hopes raised again, I hopped down, "Let me show you—"

But she waved me off. "I know it's empty."

I doubted she knew that the refrigerator was almost totally bare. It was never that way at Ted and Mandy's, even when Mandy forgot to stop by the grocery store. Always something in the fridge or the cabinets. You might not like dill pickles and crackers, but they were something to eat. Here, the fridge had a six-pack of pomegranate juice, a six-pack of light beer, and a small jar of green olives. Not the good black olives, but the green ones with something red stuffed into them.

It wasn't much of a supper, pomegranate juice and stuffed green olives.

Miss Porter jerked open her leather briefcase and rummaged around. Then she snapped it shut, her long red fingernails almost catching in the latch. "Sorry. I only have a debit card. I never keep cash anymore."

Almost desperate now, I flung open the refrigerator. "There's nothing here."

"I told my brother to stop by the store the day before you came, but he was too busy, helping get that back to school party ready." She paused. "Oh, I meant to bring in something."

She went out the back door to her car and brought back a large flat white box. "Leftovers from today's luncheon." She slid the box onto the counter and opened it. About 100 cream puffs, tiny ones. They smelled sweet and I saw that some had chocolate, some vanilla filling.

"Eat what you want. Sorry, but I have to go. I've just got five minutes to get there. When my brother gets home, ask him to get you a burger, and he can shop tomorrow." Miss Porter opened the back door and strode calmly to her car.

Now, cream puffs are good. But they aren't a supper.

I jerked open cabinet doors, searching. Not even a box of cereal or a can of soup. After 48 hours with the Porters as foster parents, as the succedaneum for my own parents: (Succedaneum: Latin derivation. Definition: a substitute. S-u-c-c-e-d-a-n-e-u-m. The 2001 winning word for the national spelling bee.)

Here's the progress report on the Porters:

Good–no one was going to bother me much here.

Good–No chores because they hired a maid to come once a week, they both ate out most of the time, Mr. Porter took his shirts and pants–and my school uniform–to a laundry service.

Bad–I was truly on my own. Including where I would get my supper tonight.

I leaned over the cold kitchen counter and ate a chocolate cream puff. It was fresh and soft, and the pudding was a deep chocolate. I ate another.

According to Miss Porter, who liked to explain her brother, I was here because of their feud. Mr. versus Miss Porter, brother versus sister. They had lived in this house together for years. Miss Porter was divorced, and her only son, Tim, graduated last May and went to college this fall on a golf scholarship. He traveled with his dad all summer, so his room had been empty for three months, and that had started arguments.

Mr. Porter: We have this big empty house and some poor foster child needs a home. Besides, I miss Tim.

Miss Porter: I've raised a son. I don't want any more kids. But if you want to do it, go ahead. I dare you.

It was the dare, of course, that made Mr. Porter go through with the application process and the first training session. Because of the dare, I was here.

I slammed shut every cabinet door. Feeling distinctly forlorn, I flopped in front of the huge screen TV with the box of cream puffs and my picture album and started flipping channels. At least Mandy had made sure that I had an album with all my pictures; I hadn't had to search for them. It was red leather outside, and pictures were slipped into plastic sleeves. Nothing labeled, but it looked like it was all in order, staring with first grade.

Let me say: sitting alone and eating junk food and looking at old pictures of your old family is not fun. By 8 p.m., two empty pomegranate juice bottles and a half empty box of cream puffs sat on the table in front of me. I had eaten all the chocolate-filled ones.

A car pulled up in the driveway, and a car door slammed. I went to the kitchen to meet Mr. Porter.

"Hey." Mr. Porter waved good-bye to someone in a black car, then stepped inside. He nodded toward the living room. "You watching something good?"

"No. Just waiting for you to come home for supper?"

His eyebrows went up and his jaw dropped a bit. "Oh." He shrugged. "Well, I ate a burger at the bowling alley." He walked through the kitchen to the living room.

As he passed me, I wrinkled my nose. He smelled like beer or wine or something.

Seeing the box on the table, he leaned over, took a cream puff and popped it into his mouth. "Looks like you had dessert already. Too bad she didn't bring home any chocolate ones; they are the best."

My throat tightened. Did these Porters understand nothing? "Yes, that's all I had to eat. The refrigerator is empty. The cabinets are empty. Can we just drive through somewhere and get me a burger? Please."

"No," he said. "Can't go out again. I had two beers and caught a ride home. Designated driver, ya know what I mean? Left my car at the bowling alley."

Well, at least he didn't drink and drive. That was good.

"Tonight," he said, "was my last chance at some fun before I have to spend evenings grading papers. Ya know what I mean? Just fix yourself something." He burped.

I had been neglected all evening, left alone with the cream puffs, and I was about to be mad. I said in a calm voice. "Maybe we could order a pizza? Have it delivered?"

He dropped onto the couch. Obviously–not listening. He stared at me for a minute, his eyes unblinking. Then he lay down, curled up and closed his eyes. And just like that, my chance of a pizza disappeared.

I grabbed my picture album and stomped upstairs to my room and stood in the doorway, thinking again how much I hated this room, Tim's room. Along one wall was a putting green. Tim, like Mr. Porter, was crazy about golf. Was going to college on a golf scholarship, they said. Mr. Porter supposedly had a putting green in his bedroom and one in his classroom at school, too.

Worst thing about my room? The leftover smells. Dirty socks smell. Heavy cologne smells. UFO smells. Foul, that's what it was, both the smell and how the Porters had treated me tonight. I kicked off my shoes and lay stiffly on top of the covers and turned off the lamp. I crossed my arms over my chest, but then I had to hold my nose. My stomach hurt, so I tried patting it softly, but then I had to hold my nose. I was so miserable: I had chocolate-pomegranate breath, and I just wanted a bag of chips. That wasn't asking much. Just a small bag of salty chips.

I should have just gone to sleep. But even more than the hunger was the worry about Mandy and her baby.

When I got here, the social worker and Mr. Porter both said I shouldn't try to call Mandy. But that was crazy. Well, Mr. Porter would be asleep for hours now.

I went to the hallway and picked up the house phone. Quickly, before I could think about it, I called the familiar number.

And Ted answered, "Hello."

I tried to make my voice deep, "Mandy Payne, please."

There was a pause. Then Ted said, "Alli, I know it's you."

I was quiet. He had never liked my voice, always telling me to talk softer. At first, I tried talking quietly, or even whispering, but that wasn't what he meant. "Your voice is harsh. Can you make it softer?"

I never figured out what he meant or how to change my voice.

Before he could yell at me for calling, I hung up.

I went back and lay on my hard bed, on an itchy blanket, quivering with rage. Home. What did Ted know about a home?

I should have just gone to sleep. But I was eleven and a half years old. Almost twelve. And teenagers NEVER got adopted. Everybody knows that.

Somehow, I knew–had known for a long time–Ted and Mandy wouldn't adopt me, but that had been okay because I would still live with them, and not have to move until I graduated from high school. But now–

I took the red album and buried it under my clothes, where I wouldn't have to look at it again. I had to take care of myself. No adults to help.

I just wanted one small bag of potato chips. After endless cream puffs, something salty.

Well, I was going to eat something more than cream puffs tonight. Somewhere. Right now. I got up and groped around for my shoes and put them on.

ELIOT

Cradling the container of sourdough starter, I followed Marj back into the living room for our serious talk, glad the suspense was almost over. Marj sat on the sofa; I perched on the other end.

Marj rubbed her temples with her thumbs and sighed. She slipped off her flip-flops, then pulled up her bony knees and hugged them, her chin resting on her knees, staring at me. "We need to talk."

I caught myself drumming the side of the jar and forced my fingers to be still. I waited.

"You saw the envelope." A statement, not a question.

I nodded and hugged the jar–a cold, hard security blanket.

"You probably guessed, it's the adoption papers. I just don't know what to do."

I looked at her face, but she dropped her gaze. "Sign them?" I whispered, but too soft for her to hear.

"Without Griff," she said, "everything is so hard. I've never been a mother. Never even owned a house before. Just lived in apartment complexes. There, if anything goes wrong, you call the manager, and it gets fixed. And you never worry about grass." She waved toward the back yard. "That grass out there–" she sighed deeply and sagged, "– it never stops growing."

A warm flush swept through me, and I was embarrassed I hadn't thought to do the mowing. "Grass? Is that what's bothering you? I can mow. Right now, if you want. I can keep that done. Yard work, I can do that. I swear, I can keep it all done."

Marj grimaced. "No, it's not just that."

Now, I set the sourdough jar between my feet and sat on my hands to make sure I was quiet. She liked it when I was quiet and listened.

"You know that Griff and I were high school sweethearts?"

I nodded, interested as always in Griff's background, his life.

"But we lost track of each other," she continued. "I married someone else. Jack was, well, he was great, but we couldn't have children. And then, he got cancer and died four years ago."

"Oh." That I hadn't known. Griff just said he met his high school sweetheart and wanted to date her again. Nothing about a first husband, especially one who had died of cancer.

"When I met Griff again," Marj said, "it was like a dream. He was so strong and confident. With Griff beside me, I felt like I could climb Mt. Everest."

Oh, yes, I knew that feeling.

She stopped talking, so I risked a glance. Her eyes were half closed, and she was half smiling; then, her brow wrinkled and she squeezed her eyes tight, like she was trying not to cry.

Yes, I thought, memories of Griff were hard. But good.

Squinting, Marj whispered, "I don't know anything right now. Except that everything is difficult with Griff gone. And I didn't count on being the single mom of a twelve-year-old boy. Without Griff, well—" she hesitated.

I looked away, staring at the dark TV screen. I waited.

"—well, maybe it would be best to stop before we get started."

"But. We're a family." Her words stung, but I couldn't think about the hurt. I had to make her understand that we had to stay together. We had been a family for four weeks. Marj and Griff married early that summer and took a two-week honeymoon. When they came back, we all had a week together before Griff got sick. That week, we had filed papers for Marj to officially adopt me, too.

"Are we? A family?" Marj shook her head and sat up, planting her feet on the ground and leaning forward to speak with a firm voice. "Don't think me harsh. This is just more than I ever expected and I'm not ready to be a single mom. I've already talked with your old social worker and explained my hesitation. They are experts in children; they'll know what to do. They said you could move to a foster family this fall. They have a family ready for a boy. A really nice family. Who will know how to take care of you much better than I can. They are experts in children."

Confusion swirled around me. Marj believed what she was saying, that I'd be better off with a foster family. It was true, in some ways. Marj didn't know things about kids, like not even thinking about giving me an allowance. But she had no idea how bad foster care could be. From between my feet, I picked up the sourdough jar, unscrewed the top and leaned over for a deep breath. And time stood still.

Home. The sharp smell of sourdough always brought memories of Griff. On one of my first visits to Griff's house, four years ago, when I was just a foster child for another couple, we made our first loaf of bread together. It was a long holiday for Presidents' Day in February. My foster family went on a family trip, so Griff invited me to stay over. Friday night, Griff pulled a glass jar from the fridge. "Ever make bread?"

I tapped the jar, puzzled. It seemed to be full of a yellowish-white liquid with foam on top. "No. Doesn't bread just come from the store?"

Griff launched into a big lecture on sourdough. He was like that, knew so much about science and the world. Loved explaining things. Not like lecturing from a teacher, so much as giving me a gift of knowledge.

Griff's voice still echoes in me, like echoes from a booming voice would linger for a long time in a canyon: Sourdough, he said, is made from a combination of yeast and bacteria. The yeast gives off gases that makes the bread light and fluffy. The bacteria gives it a sour taste. Today, most breads rise too fast and the bacteria doesn't have time to develop that sour flavor.

Taking off the lid, he held out the jar.

I took a whiff. "Stinks."

"Heavenly smell," Griff said and grinned that huge grin that showed his one false tooth in the front of his mouth. "Kinda like dirty socks."

That smell, that amazing smell, followed us all weekend as the bread rose, was punched down, and rose again. Finally the loaf came out of the oven, and Griff slathered it with real butter and handed it to me.

I chewed and considered.

"Well?" Griff demanded.

I made him wait, taking another bite and leaning my head from side to side.

"Well?"

I gave in and giggled. "Heavenly," I said, using Griff's word.

And Griff beamed, lighting up a place in my heart that I thought would never be lit by anyone again.

Suddenly, I thought of Alli, living with the Porters. I could not go back to being a foster child, I could not.

Panic rose now, and I breathed faster. Marj had to understand. She had to give us more time. Time. Griff would understand: it took him two years to decide to adopt me. Taking time to make a decision was fine, as long as Marj and I stuck it out and tried. Griff had truly loved Marj, and that meant she was a good person. We just needed time.

I screwed the lid back on the jar. Then stared at it like I had never seen if before. A minute ago, the Bread Project had seemed impossible, almost a thing that would disrespect Griff. Something that would leave me exposed, hold my grief up for everyone to see. But maybe Dad had left me one last thing, a way to convince Marj to give us time, time to get to know each other, time to become a family.

I looked up and blurted, "What about the Bread Project? We want to make it work, right? To honor Griff and his memory. Right? We have to work together. You work with the PTA, and I get the kids excited. Right?"

Marj opened her mouth, and then shut it.

Maybe she was rethinking her decision. I pressed harder. "The Bread Project has to succeed. For Griff's sake, we have to see it through. Together. Right? Through Thanksgiving. We can't change anything until after Thanksgiving. At least. Right?"

"O-k-a-y," she said slowly, reluctantly. "I do want the Bread Project to be a success. We could wait until Thanksgiving to decide something about the foster family."

My shoulders sagged in relief. Time. We had time. A chance at Marj as a real mother–it was worth people poking around in my feelings. The final success or failure of the Project–well, it would probably fail but that didn't matter. What I really needed was as much time as possible. But this was going to be tricky. The Project would be like a time bomb that would go off when the timer stopped. I had to keep winding the clock. The Bread Project had to start well and keep going.

And in that space of time, from now to Thanksgiving, I had to convince Marj that we were family, that she should sign those papers.

"But I really don't know what to do with a house like this." Her voice was brisk again. "I met Mr. and Mrs. Johnson at the party yesterday. They paint and fix up houses. We set up an appointment to look things over and get an estimate. Get it ready to sell. We'll go on and do that. It will make it easier to move on—if that's what we decide." She saw that I was about to speak, so she raised a hand. "Like Mrs. Lopez said, it's still hard for me to make decisions. I get so sad sometimes—" She trailed off and squeezed her eyes shut again.

"No big decisions right now then," I said quickly. "And I'll do better about helping. With everything. You'll see." I loved this old house, but that wasn't as important as keeping the family together. I would gladly move if only Marj would stick it out.

Marj rubbed her temples again.

Quickly, I asked, "You need some headache medicine? A glass of iced tea?"

"No, I'm fine. Just need to be a couch potato for a while."

"You want me to take this sourdough over to Alli?" Suddenly, I needed to talk to Alli.

Marj nodded. "Explain it all to her again. And be back in an hour or so." She stretched out on the couch and reached for the TV remote.

I ran upstairs for shoes and was soon marching toward the Porter's house. The Bread Project had just bought me twelve weeks to change Marj's mind about putting me in foster care, three short months for us to learn how to be a family together.

Step One: make dead sure Alli still supported the Bread Project and would help make it a smashing success.

The evening was hot and sticky, the late summer still heating up into the 90s during the day, and not cooling off until midnight. I strode quickly to the Porter's house, my flip-flops rhythmically slapping the sidewalk. The plastic jar with sourdough starter was lightweight, but rehearsing the arguments for the Bread Project, I felt heavy, dragged down. Alli already liked the idea of the Bread Project, though, so maybe this would be easy.

Half a block away from the Porter's house, the upstairs light went off, the only light in the house. I almost turned around and went home, thinking everyone had gone to bed early, and I'd have to deliver the sourdough starter tomorrow.

Squee! The upstairs window opened with a loud protest. Probably hadn't been opened in years. Following the sound, I spotted her. Alli was leaning out of the upstairs window.

I hated the Porter's house. First time I went there with Griff, Mr. Porter bragged, "This house is on the Historic Register. Oldest on our street, a modern-style house of the 1950s."

You ask me? It was ugly. Made of concrete that might have been white when it was built, but had turned a muddy gray. Besides, the whole thing was too square. Only one good thing about it. The trees and shrubs were so overgrown, they hid the actual house from view.

Alli reached for a tree limb, grabbed hold, and then swung out.

She was sneaking out?

Her legs hung a minute before she pulled them up to wrap over the branch. She hitched herself closer to the trunk, till she could set her feet on a branch just below. Quickly, she dropped to the ground.

Why was she doing this? She'd only been with the Porters for a couple days. You didn't want to get in trouble that fast. Not without a very good reason.

I could have said her name, made her stop. But curiosity won: where was she going?

I stashed the plastic jar of sourdough in the bushes and followed.

The Porter's neighborhood was older, but richer than mine, the yards all picture perfect like in a magazine. It was a pleasant neighborhood for an evening walk.

I kept a block away from Alli, tailing her like a P.I. on TV. It was a thought that made me smirk at myself.

Alli turned two rights, heading toward a main street. Where was she going?

She turned off into an alley and crossed the road into the parking lot of a grocery store. I debated what to do, but finally decided to wait outside.

Waiting, I counted sixteen carts of bagged groceries, three bicyclists dropping coins in the machine outside the front door for Gatorade, five men coming out with a single bag–probably Hungry Man dinners–and one old lady who tottered along on too-high heels, and I ran to help her carry a watermelon to her car. She tipped me a whole dollar. Nice neighborhood.

By then, I was bored. Time to find Alli.

I walked into the store, blinking at the sudden bright lights. And there was Alli, just slipping under the security gates at the opposite door.

Beep! Beep! Beep! The security alarm blared.

A uniformed guard grabbed Alli's arm. "Hey, kid. Where you going? What did you steal?"

Alli's eyes bulged large, scared. She held a small bag of chips. Just potato chips, plain, nothing special.

Heart pounding, I reacted instinctively—knowing even as I did it that I'd regret it later. I ran toward Alli and the guard and stopped in front of them. "Sis, I said I'd be right in to pay." I tried to sound angry.

Alli just stared at me.

"Sorry, officer, I was just trying to lock up our bikes, and then I was coming in to pay." I pulled out the one-dollar tip I had just gotten. "See?"

"Hmmm." The guard wore three gold rings on the hand that held Alli, and he wore a thick gold chain. "You're brother and sister?"

Once you start lying, you have to keep on. I punched Alli's thin shoulder. "We fight like brother and sister, believe me."

Still, the gold-rings-hand didn't turn loose of Alli. He must work here, I thought, to pay for his bling. He didn't really care about the store; I just needed to bluff him.

"Different mothers," I said, trying to think fast. Then, before the guard could say more, I pulled the chips from Alli's hands, walked over to the self-serve station, swiped the bar codes, stashed the chips in a plastic bag, and fed my hard-earned money into the machine.

Alli was still mute, a small miracle, but now, the guard had let her go. I marched past her, grabbed her arm myself, and dragged her out with me. She was smart enough not to resist—after all, I was saving her. Without looking back, we hit the open air and ran. Didn't stop till we were two blocks away.

I held up the grocery bag. "Okay, explain."

"Why should I to explain to you?"

"Because I just saved you."

"I was hungry."

I groaned. Porter wasn't feeding her? "You're being stupid. Do what Porter asks and you'll get fed."

Alli jerked the grocery bag away from me and hung it on her arm while she opened the chips bags and started stuffing it in. "You don't understand. I don't have any chores at all." Through loud crunchy bites, she explained about the maid, the eating out and the laundry. "Got everything covered, except Mr. Porter misses his nephew, who went off to college this year on a golf scholarship. Thought he needed another kid. Except he's not used to a kid who needs to eat."

"What does that mean?"

"There's no food in the house. Well. Six bottles of pomegranate juice and a jar of stuffed green olives. Well. Four bottles of pomegranate juice, now. And Miss Porter brought home 100 cream puffs from some fancy party."

"Ugh. I hate pomegranate juice, but cream puffs are good."

"Yeah, the first five or six are good. The next dozen can make you sick of them."

"Okay." I reached in and took a chip. "But why steal? You get an allowance from the state. Right?"

"The first check will come later this week. But Mr. Porter has already said I don't get an allowance."

I studied her thin face. "How did you say you wound up in foster care? What happened to your dad?"

"State couldn't find him. Not after he got out of the army."

"Did you ever try to find him?" I asked. "Surely with the Internet, you could look for him. If he's still alive."

"Me? No. He didn't care enough to find me, so why should I look for him?"

"To get out of this."

"He should look for me." Her voice was hard now. She shook out the last of the chip crumbs and licked the salt from her hands. "I think Mr. Porter will buy groceries tomorrow. I hope."

"And after that, what else will he forget to do for you?" I was really, really, really going to regret this. And suddenly everything about Marj swept back over me. My parents had been unwed teenagers. They gave me up for adoption right away. There I was a nice new baby, and I should have been adopted by a nice family who really wanted me. Instead, for some reason that no one told me, the first family didn't adopt me. At age two, I had to move to a new house and a year later to another and two years later to another. I blinked hard, and took a deep breath. "I can help. But I want something in return."

Alli's brow wrinkled. "You want me to mess up the Bread Project. Right?"

"No." I had to be careful what I said here. "I changed my mind. The Project is a good way to honor my dad. I need you to help make the Bread Project a success."

Now, she stared. "Yeah, right."

I started walking down the sidewalk, back toward the Porters, avoiding her doubt. "It's true. I was just scared to try before." I chewed my bottom lip, aware of how weak that sounded.

"Really," she said. "What happened?"

Maybe she would understand. Maybe another foster kid was the only one who would understand. But I still couldn't explain. "Look, Griff, my dad thought up this project. But he died this summer." I tried to swallow, trying to bottle up my feelings. To get time with Marj, I had to make this project work. But I didn't have to hang my feelings out for everyone to see. That part was for me alone and I would shove away anyone who tried to see inside. "Marj thinks this is a good way to honor him. We talked tonight and now I understand her better, and I agree. We need this project."

She stopped under a streetlight. "You wanna try that again. What really happened?" Then, her head snapped around to look directly at me, her eyes glittering in the streetlight. "Oh. You called her Marj, not Mom. You are a foster child, too."

Funny how foster kids recognize each other. Nothing on the outside to say I'd been a foster kid. But you can feel it. Maybe it's something about the hunger on our faces when other kids talked about family.

I clenched a fist to keep it from trembling. "No, I'm not a foster kid. Griff adopted me this year."

"And with Griff gone, Marj isn't sure she wants to adopt you."

When Alli said it so bluntly like that, it sounded even worse. I ducked my head and shoved my hands in my shorts pocket and walked, the slap of my flip-flops echoing my bouncing emotions. Anger. Longing. Anger. Longing.

Alli was matching my stride again, when she clutched her stomach, and I heard it growl. Suddenly, she burped. An innocent burp.

We looked at each other and suddenly, we both laughed.

"Look, Sis, it's easy," I finally said. "I make sure you get back-up in dealing with the Porters. Food. Whatever you need. And you help me make the Bread Project work."

"Done." Alli stuck out her hand to shake. "I get help when I need it. You get help on the Bread Project."

My arms were frozen to my side. Could I trust her?

Impatient, she said, "You think I don't care about anything, but you're wrong. Decent food is my goal today. And tomorrow. Just making it through one day at a time, that's my goal."

If Alli had said she cared about my problems, I wouldn't trust her. But making it through one day at a time was an honest thing. "Done," I agreed and shook her hand.

BREAD PROJECT: WEEK 1

ELIOT

I can't remember a time when I wasn't trying to please someone.

Well, maybe with Griff—I didn't have to try to keep him happy. Maybe if Griff was still here, I wouldn't be trying so hard to please Marj. Because I was trying very, very, very hard to please her.

That night, Friday night, I set my alarm for 6 a.m.

For four hours before Marj got up, I worked in the yard. Quietly. Using Griff's old push mower.

"It's slower," Griff told me the first time we did yard work together, "but it cuts clean, and the grass grows better." He spent an afternoon teaching me how to sharpen the blades.

By 9 a.m., I had all the lawn cut, the shrubs trimmed, and the leaf litter from the flowerbeds bagged. I even cleared out the vines and mess at the back of the yard, something Griff had meant to do this summer. I picked up all the foliage and bagged it, too, while slapping at bugs and scratching where they bit. Finally, I stacked all the bags by the front curb and went in to shower.

By 10 a.m., I smelled like soap. I scrambled eggs, toasted English muffins and made coffee. Then I put three rose buds–the last of the summer–and a length of vine in a vase and arranged it all on a tray. I tiptoed to Marj's room and knocked.

"Come in." Then, leaning up on an elbow, Marj asked, "What's this?"

I used my most cheerful voice. "Saturday morning breakfast." And I watched her carefully. Would this please her?

"Well. Thank you." Marj yawned, then rubbed her eyes, then rubbed her nose, like she was trying to rub off freckles. She stretched, stood, opened the window curtains, and sat on the window seat in her pajamas, blinking at the bright light. I put the breakfast tray on the nearby table and sat in the extra chair and watched.

Marj sipped coffee, then looked outside. She glanced at me, and then back outside.

"You do all that?" She waved at the tidy yard.

"Yes." Nervous, I waited for reaction.

"Wow, it looks great. Thanks."

Her words weren't much, but her face relaxed, and she smiled directly at me. It made me smile right back. Pleased that she was pleased.

"When did you do it? Why didn't I hear you? I would have come out and helped."

I explained about Griff's push mower and the hand tools for cutting shrubs. "I can do the yard work myself."

Marj's forehead wrinkled, but she said nothing.

I wanted to press her right then, to get her to say that if I kept up the yard work, she'd try to make things work. But I had learned: never push an adult into a corner when they might say, "No." Better to wait.

I had done enough that morning.

"Well, I'm going to watch cartoons. May I ask a couple friends to come over this afternoon and practice baking bread? For the Bread Project?"

Marj blinked, still looking sleepy. "Not today. But tomorrow afternoon, after church. Whatever time you want."

ALLI

Friday night, Mr. Porter abandoned me again. Left me at home watching TV while he went to the grocery store. Wouldn't let me go and pick out things. At last, the refrigerator had milk, juice, and lunch meat. The cabinets had lots of cans and boxes, things I'd look at later when Mr. Porter wasn't watching. Just hoped I'd find something I liked.

Saturday morning, two things happened. First, Miss Brodie-Rock, the social worker, stopped by unexpectedly. Mr. Porter was lucky that he'd just bought groceries.

Visits from the social worker were supposed to happen about once a month. But the old social worker, Mrs. Thatcher, trusted Ted and Mandy, so after the first year, she only came by three or four times a year. I liked her; she listened.

Miss Brodie-Rock was large. Chubby-cheeked. But she dressed in a dark business suit and high heels. Professional, she said. She was pretty with perfect hair, perfect nails. But she didn't listen.

Mr. Porter had given her a tour of the house, and now we both sat on the kitchen bar stools while Mr. Porter sat at the kitchen table reading his newspaper and drinking coffee and barely listening to us.

And Miss Brodie-Rock was getting down to business. "What's this about you calling the Paynes?"

"I only wanted to know if Mandy was okay," I explained.

"I can tell you, Mrs. Payne is fine."

"But after the fall, is Mandy okay? Is the baby okay?"

"Everything is fine. Mrs. Payne is feeling fine." Miss Brodie-Rock tapped her ink pen on her clipboard. "But you're not. The Paynes asked you not to call. You called. So, now, this phone number—" She pointed to the house phone on the kitchen counter "—is blocked. The call won't go through."

Ted worked for a telecom company and could easily do things like block phone numbers. He'd done it before for a man he had to fire. I shouldn't be surprised he did it now. But just now, I longed to hear Mandy, hear her say anything. I would even have loved to hear Mandy scolding me because I hadn't folded my clothes. Or, because I hadn't put my milk glass in the dishwasher. Or, because I hadn't brushed my teeth. Mandy was the only mother I knew. I had to know if she was really okay, if her baby was okay.

But Miss Brodie-Rock had moved on, checking off her list. "Are you doing your chores here?"

I started to say, "No," because I didn't have any. But—here's the thing: Mr. Porter doesn't do laundry and hasn't let me near the washer and dryer that sit in the laundry room, lonely and unused. He bought me four school uniforms and has two cleaned each week, while I wear the other two. Okay, nothing wrong with that. But socks and underwear, I only had four pair of each. He never sent those out.

When he explained this that first day, I had protested. "I can do my own laundry."

"I don't want you making messes. It's easier for me this way," Mr. Porter said. "Just wash them out by hand and hang them in your bathroom."

But hand-washed socks never get really clean.

"Well," I said to Miss Brodie-Rock, "I know I need to learn to do my own laundry. Maybe Mr. Porter can show me how to use the washer and dryer right now."

Miss Brodie-Rock beamed, her chubby cheeks getting as round and fat as tennis balls. "Excellent. I'll be able to observe you two working together." She stood up, her heels making the same satisfying click that Miss Porter's always did.

Mr. Porter glanced up, then back at his newspaper.

"Mr. Porter?" she asked. "Let's do this now, please."

"Do what?"

"You weren't listening?"

Mr. Porter looked up, apparently still engrossed in whatever he was reading. He did read the newspaper from cover to cover every morning.

Miss Brodie-Rock repeated slowly, "I'd like to observe you and Alli working together. Perhaps this would be a good time for you to teach her to use the washer and dryer."

"Oh." Still, Mr. Porter sat. "But—" He narrowed his eyes at me.

"Now, please?"

"Oh. Now?"

Miss Brodie-Rock was already clacking toward the laundry room. She stopped in the doorway. "Coming?"

Finally, Mr. Porter stood, leaving the newspaper open on the table.

Passing me, he glared. Words weren't needed. I had used Miss Brodie-Rock to get something I wanted, and he did not like it.

But a few minutes later, my school uniforms, all my socks and all but the underwear I had on were sloshing around in soap and water. I had food and now, clean clothes. Finally. Social workers were good for something.

I almost grinned. I was getting Mr. Porter into shape pretty fast.

When she left a few minutes later, Miss Brodie-Rock shook Mr. Porter's hand, "You're doing everything right, Mr. Porter. Just keep it up."

"Thank you," he said solemnly.

We stood on the front step and watched her drive away. Then Mr. Porter said in a calm, low voice, "Don't use Miss Brodie-Rock against me again. Tim always tried to get my sister and I to disagree, too, so I know the tricks you kids use. This is the only time you use that machine. Next time, you can hand wash. Go on up to your room till supper."

My face burned with embarrassment, my jaws clenched. Any reasonable person would have already taught me to use the washing machine. I just wanted clean clothes. But I had made things worse.

ELIOT

About noon on Saturday, I suddenly started itching.

Alli had reminded me that a person's hand has 1500 bacteria on every square centimeter of skin. Every time I scratched, I saw my hand as a miniature metropolis for millions of bacteria. Between my fingers was a small town, just right for a couple hundred-thousand bacteria, probably all from the same family. My hairy arms were flat, fertile fields full of bacteria, fields ready for harvest.

I tried to laugh at myself. Really, I had not itched like this for three years. I tried to tell myself that there was nothing, no germs. Instead, I itched; I scratched; I worried.

It took me back to those days in first grade when worrying about germs could send me into a panic attack. Dr. Spray had taught me techniques to avoid the attack. Gee, I hadn't thought of them for over two years. And that made me worry even more. A year without meds. I didn't want to go back.

That afternoon, I worked on the website about Griff. I downloaded pictures that people had sent, cleaned them up in Photoshop, and uploaded them to the right pages. They were mostly black and whites, but some pictures were badly faded color photos and those were hard to fix. Computer work always helped me forget about myself. I concentrated on the tiny details of making a web page, trying to position everything exactly right.

But eventually, my stomach demanded food. I went to the kitchen and fixed a peanut butter and jelly sandwich—on sourdough, of course. With the first bite, the itching started again. I stopped and washed my hands, getting rid of the germs, I was sure. All 1500 bacteria for every square centimeter.

I ate half the sandwich, nibbling off the crust first, then nibbling away at the middle. By then, I could barely hold the sandwich without twitching. Disgusted with myself, I set the sandwich on a paper towel and washed my hands again.

This time, I carried my sandwich back upstairs to my computer, as far away from the sink as I could. Passing Marj's office door, she leaned away from her computer and watched me, but said nothing.

I wish she had stopped me to talk, but what did we have to talk about?

Upstairs, I quickly finished the sandwich, forcing myself to take big bites.

I needed distractions. I called Toby and invited him to bake bread the next day. And I kept him on the line talking about his PeeWee football practice that morning.

When Toby finally hung up, I debated about calling Alli. The thing is, yesterday, when given a choice, Alli took a regular Band-Aid. Miss Clay had laid out neon-colored, camo, cutesy Barbie or GI-Joe, or just the plain skin-colored bandages. Why did she still do that for sixth graders? Alli took a skin-colored one. And she didn't want a huge one, but one just the right size. The other girls in our class hadn't outgrown the habit of choosing strange ones. Marissa Blue always wanted the neon colors; Patsy Rupert went for the cutesy things; and Julie Apple, well, she got the biggest, loudest Band-Aid offered. Such babies.

Maybe Alli would be okay to work with on the Bread Project, not flashy or giggly or silly like the other girls. I could try her out by inviting her to the house with Toby. If she was okay here, she might work out. I took a big breath and dialed the Porters. When Alli said, "Yes," I said, "Thanks, bye."

I was calm enough to go the kitchen and pull out the sourdough starter and mix up some dough. I concentrated on the dough, on measuring the flour, on stirring the thick dough with a spoon, trying not to get sidetracked. Trying not to think of germs and soap.

I set the dough bowl into the oven to proof. By tomorrow morning, it would be double in size and ready to make bread with Toby and Alli. Then I fed the remaining starter and put it back in the refrigerator.

Marj wandered into the kitchen, rummaging the shelves in search of pretzels, coming up with some cheese crackers. She was scratching her arm, too.

Dr. Spray had even explained why people around me might be scratching, too. It was "sympathetic itching." Marj was scratching because I was scratching. Probably didn't even know she was doing it.

Finally, I tried Dr. Spray's most effective technique: I tried to make the itching feel even worse. Griff had explained: He said I had to believe it was in my head before the relaxation thing would work.

"My stomach itches," I told myself.

Well, yes. It did.

"My back itches," I told myself.

It did. Everywhere itched! Despair settled in, and I sat on a kitchen stool and slumped over, laying my itchy face on the cool cabinet top.

Marj set down her glass of Coke and squinted at my neck. "Let me see." She pulled up the back of my T-shirt. "You've got a rash."

"Rash?" I didn't understand.

"You're all broken out."

"I am?"

"Don't sound so happy about it," Marj said. She opened the kitchen cabinet where medicines were kept and pulled out the Benadryl. "Maybe you're allergic to something in the yard, doing all that work this morning."

Relief flooded through me. It wasn't the anxiety coming back; it was only a rash. I wasn't going crazy. "I have a rash." I smiled at Marj, then swallowed the pill she handed me and drank a glass of water.

I had gotten up early that morning, so I was already tired. The Benadryl put me to sleep so soundly that I didn't wake until the middle of Sunday morning, when Marj shook me awake.

"Look." She thrust her hand in my face.

"What?" I shoved into a sitting position and squinted, trying to focus. Marj's hand had clear blisters on two fingers. "What?" I repeated.

"Poison ivy."

"No way!"

"That vine, the one you put in the flower vase? Poison ivy. I didn't pay attention until I threw it out this morning."

I collapsed backwards and pulled the pillow over my face. All that yard work. And now, things would be even worse. Marj was never a good patient, one of her few faults Griff used to tease.

"It's okay, Eliot." Marj had a grudging tone. "It was an accident."

I peeked out. She looked tired, like a deflated tire. "I'm sorry," I whispered.

"It's okay." She studied her other hand, then held it up to show me a blister on it, too. "We won't go to church today. I'm going to the pharmacy."

After she left, I hugged the pillow to my stomach and realized that I wanted to scratch my arms, my legs, my back, my face–everywhere. I just stared at the ceiling, trying not to itch, trying not to cry, trying not to think of how stupid I had been to bring her poison ivy.

Trying not to think. 1500 bacteria. Every square centimeter.

ALLI

Tall oaks, white two-story house, green roof, big porch, green front door–I loved Eliot's house on sight. I wiped my sweaty hands on my shorts, and then pushed the doorbell. Eliot sounded nervous yesterday when he called. Like he wasn't sure he wanted to invite me over. I'd have to make sure I did everything right. I needed him as my backup for the Porters. Inside, the chimes rang. Everything was so traditional, so homey.

Eliot led me into a large kitchen that was open to a living room beyond. Toby was wearing a sloppy T-shirt, worn-out shorts and flip-flops. Pouring himself a glass of milk, making himself at home. I was so glad I had washed clothes that morning and had changed into clean shorts and a T-shirt.

Mrs. Winston was in the living room on a leather couch, reading. I knew my etiquette, thanks to Mandy. I went straight to Mrs. Winston and held out a hand to shake. "Thank you, for letting me come over."

She looked up from her book, and I stopped, startled. Her face reminded me of Miss Brodie-Rock's tennis ball cheeks, it was that swollen. She held up her hands and shrugged at me.

If her face was bad, her hands were worse, with blisters and pukey-pink medicine. I jerked my hand away and hid it behind my back.

"You're welcome. But I can't shake. Eliot and I both got into some poison ivy yesterday." She nodded curtly. "Just make yourself at home."

"Thank you," I repeated. And wondered how they got into poison ivy: leaves of three, leave them be. It was easy to spot. Bet Eliot got in trouble for that one.

In the kitchen, Eliot had a blue bowl set out. He held up his hands and said, "It has to be kneaded one more time. But I can't do it."

He had disgusting hands, too. On him, the pukey-pink poison ivy lotion had dried up, making everything blotchy. Eliot wasn't touching anything in the kitchen today. 'Cause if he did? I wouldn't eat.

Toby grinned at me. "Do you know how to knead?"

"Nope."

Eliot used air-motions to show us how to fold over the dough and push it away. "You just keep doing that. Okay, who wants to start?"

Well, I wanted to make friends and that meant I should try it first. Eliot made me wash my hands before starting. But when I finished, he said, "Wash them again."

I washed again, except this time, Eliot handed me a small nail brush and watched me scrub. To keep from saying something I shouldn't, I sucked in my cheeks until I dried my hands.

Finally, he scooped out a cup of flour and sprinkled it onto the kitchen counter. Good thing the cup had a long handle, so he didn't have to touch any flour. Or I wouldn't have been able to stay quiet.

Toby helped me scrape out the dough, and finally, I was ready to knead: my floury hands hung over the lump of dough. Then I asked the wrong question: "How long do I have to knead it?"

Eliot had a streak of flour across his left cheek. Before he spoke, he looked away. "Not long, ten, maybe fifteen minutes. Long enough for the dough to get elastic."

I studied his face, the hair falling over his eyes. He couldn't look straight at me, so something was wrong. "Yeah, right. How long?"

"Maybe a bit longer."

"Like thirty minutes?"

"Maybe."

Suddenly, I didn't care if he got mad. "That's it." I brushed flour off my hands and washed them for the third time. "I'm not doing this. I'll get stuck doing it every time, without any help."

Eliot stared at me, and then lifted his hands. "Well, I can't do it."

"I don't care, I'll do it," Toby said. He even sounded cheerful about it. He picked up Marj's apron, a red one with a teddy bear on it, and tied it on. "I like making pottery; I bet I'll like this."

So, Eliot and I sat on stools and watched Toby play with the bread dough. He was football-strong. Even his fingers were strong: punching, kneading, shaping. Adding flour when the dough got sticky, even without Eliot telling him. He fell into a hypnotic rhythm, pulling and folding the dough over, then pushing it away from him, making a quarter-turn, then repeating. I don't know where he learned that quarter-turn trick. But it worked.

I was glad I had refused to do it. Toby was a natural.

My stomach growled, but softly. Mr. Porter had slept late that morning and so had I. When he heard I was coming to see Eliot, he called a friend and invited him for lunch and golf. Should have made a sandwich: there was still some American cheese in the fridge. But I didn't want anything then. Now, smelling the dough, I was hungry.

I hopped down to butter the loaf pans that Eliot had set out. "How long before we eat this bread?"

"It has to rise a while, then bake for an hour."

"Oh." I sucked in my cheeks, angry at myself for not eating earlier.

Eliot noticed my distress. "Marj," he called, "may I open the chips and salsa?"

"Well–" Mrs. Winston sat forward where we could see her better, grimacing at even this small movement, and started to scratch at her hands. She looked down, stopped the scratching and frowned. "It was for supper tomorrow."

"I'll pick up some more on the way home from school," Eliot said. But he patted his back pocket and frowned.

Mrs. Winston shrugged and sank back on the couch. "Okay. Sure. But leave the pretzels for me, please."

The phone rang. Neither Mrs. Winston nor Eliot wanted to answer it, and Toby's hands were full.

Mrs. Winston leaned forward again and called, "Get that, please."

I looked around and found the phone on the corner of the cabinet. It was a cordless phone, black. I grabbed the hand receiver from the base unit. "Hello?" I said.

It was Mrs. Lopez, wanting to talk about the Bread Project, so I carried the phone in to Mrs. Winston. But she had me explain about her hands and promised to call Mrs. Lopez tomorrow. Back in the kitchen, I set the receiver back in its base. And I thought of Miss Brodie-Rock that morning, tapping her clipboard and pointing at the Porter's phone. Mr. Porter's phone number was blocked from calling the Paynes.

But this one wasn't.

"Is this about ready?" Holding the dough in both hands, Toby pulled the dough up, letting it droop in the middle. It was smooth and shiny. When Eliot agreed it was ready, Toby shaped it and set the loaves in the buttered pans. Finally, we set the bread pans on top of the stove to rise.

In the breakfast room off the side of the kitchen, Eliot sat out chips, salsa and glasses of water. And the deck of cards held together with gauze.

I should have been thinking about the bread and about playing cards and worrying about catching Eliot at cheating. But my mind was on the phone. And about Mandy and her baby. And about Ted not letting me talk to Mandy. But he often went out with golf buddies on Sunday afternoons.

We wolfed down chips and salsa until the chips were almost gone and my stomach felt better.

Toby picked up the cards and said, "What do you want to play?"

"Rummy," Eliot and I said in unison.

And I smiled, knowing it was going to be a fun afternoon. But first–"Excuse me for a minute. Where's the bathroom?"

Eliot told me how to find the half bath near the door to the garage. As I went through the kitchen, I grabbed the portable phone.

In the bathroom, heart thumping, I locked the door and stood with my back against it, hugging the phone to my chest. Was I going to risk it?

Yes. Ted was gone almost every Sunday afternoon.

I held out the phone and punched in the familiar number. It rang. Once. Twice. A third time. Fourth ring–a soft voice answered, one I didn't recognize, "Hello."

"Is Mandy there?"

"Who's calling?"

"A friend. Melanie," I lied. "I just heard she had an accidental fall and wanted to know how her baby is doing."

"Oh, that's sweet. This is her mother, Mimi Holt. She spent two days in the hospital, and they say the baby is fine, but I'm going to be here until the baby comes. They still want her to stay in bed, but she's fine."

"Oh, good. I just wanted an update."

"Oh, for updates. Ted is starting a blog about the baby," Mimi said. "It's BabyPayne.com. Neat, huh? Oh, but still call, Mandy will want to talk to you."

"Hello." It was Ted's voice.

I clicked the phone off and slid down the door until I was sitting on the floor. My heart was thumping in my ears. Finally, I knew something solid. Mimi, Mandy's mother, lived in Houston, Texas and hadn't come up often. But she had been there a couple times for Christmas, and I knew she wouldn't lie to me. The baby was okay, really okay.

But Ted had picked up the other portable phone. Had he suspected it was me? Would he block Eliot's number, too?

Eliot! And Toby!

I stood up from the bathroom floor and unlocked the door. I wouldn't worry about Ted tracing this number or blocking it until it happened. Because now, I decided, I would read the blog every week and find out when the baby was born, and I would go to the hospital to see it, like we did for Mandy's friend, Melanie. I wouldn't bother Mandy or Ted or Mimi, just look in the nursery window at the baby. I wanted to be sure the baby was perfect, just like Mandy wanted.

Meanwhile, there was a card game I wanted to win.

What I didn't expect was that we would play for real money. That Eliot, he was clever. He didn't have enough money to share, so he was doing the next best thing: sharing his method of getting money. Sure, I had to agree to help Toby mow grass if I lost, but that was nothing.

By the time the bread came out of the oven three hours later, Eliot and I each had ten dollars, and Toby's billfold was thinner. But not empty. Playing cards with Toby might not give me an allowance every week. But it helped today.

And today? Eliot had bread to share.

That bread. Before this week, I had never heard of sourdough. For sure, never eaten it. Never had fresh-baked bread, straight from the oven. Eliot cut the largest piece for Toby. Buttered it for him, too. Served him first. After all, Toby had lost twenty dollars. You might even say that was a twenty-dollar piece of bread.

So, I didn't mind waiting. When it finally came? Wow. Sourdough bread was sour and sweet and warm. Wow.

❖

Monday morning, I dressed in my school uniform but padded to the kitchen barefoot. My school shoes were way too big and uncomfortable, so I wore them as little as possible. The kitchen was on the west side of the house, and the breakfast table, sitting in the bay window, was shaded for breakfast and hot at suppertime. Mr. Porter was already there, leaning over the kitchen counter and reading the newspaper.

I walked past him, and he started talking. "Tim did great in his golf tournament this weekend. A birdie on the first hole, par on the second. . . ."

Meant nothing to me. I didn't understand golf.

A pan of water was heating on the stove, and beside Mr. Porter was a French coffee press, a small pitcher with a built in sieve to keep coffee grounds in the pitcher and out of your cup. Mandy had liked French press coffee, too.

". . .so with two holes left, he was tied," Mr. Porter went on, "Wish I could have watched."

I fixed a bowl of cereal and poured milk on it and sat at the breakfast table to eat, wrapping one leg around the chair leg. I concentrated on the crunching sound of the cereal.

Still talking, Mr. Porter poured boiling water into the French press, and the smell of coffee filled the room. ". . .my sister called last night and told me Tim won. Wish I'd been there."

I loved the coffee smell. Hated the taste of it, though.

He opened the fridge and pulled out the milk and–

–wait, that was the sourdough starter jar.

He stood stiff, uncomfortable, holding the jar at arm's length while he moved aside something else before he pulled out the jug of milk. Worried, I raced across the cool tile floor and took the sourdough starter from his hands. "Here, I'll hold that for you."

Mr. Porter poured milk into his coffee and put the milk back in the fridge and closed the door. When he stepped aside, I opened the fridge again and put the starter on a shelf in the door, far away from the milk. The jar fit tightly on that shelf, but it did fit. Would Mr. Porter help keep it alive? Maybe it was the wrong time to ask, but I had to ask sometime. "By the way," I said casually, "I need flour for the sourdough starter. By Thursday night so I can take it back on Friday."

"You telling me when I have to shop?" he snapped.

I retreated back to the kitchen table. "No, sir."

He leaned over the paper again, his frowning face a mass of pockmarks and wrinkles.

"I was just–"

He sighed and looked sideways at me. "–just what?"

"Just trying to give you lots of notice. You know, tell you ahead of time when I might need something. That way, you could work it into your schedule."

Nodding curtly, he folded the paper and laid it beside the French press. "I just don't like this Bread Project."

"Why?"

Mr. Porter made a show of refilling his coffee cup, adding milk again, glaring at the starter in the fridge's doorway. "When Griff–Mr. Winston–started working at the school, we were both bachelors. We golfed, ate out, did a few things together."

That surprised me. Seemed like Porter was always mad at the mention of Mr. Winston; weird, since Mr. Winston was dead. I gathered my dishes, dumped out the leftover milk and put everything in the dishwasher. And waited.

"Look." Mr. Porter rubbed his hand across his eyes. "You ever have a friend who always one-ups you?"

"Oh." Suddenly, I did see. Mr. Porter had let his sister and nephew live with him. But Mr. Winston had adopted Eliot and married Mrs. Winston. Probably lots of other places they were in competition, too, things I wouldn't even guess about. Maybe scores on certain golf courses.

"But–"

"I know." Mr. Porter waved his hand, cutting me off. "Still."

I studied my feet. I rubbed my left ankle with my right foot, not daring to look at him. It was weird for an adult to admit to something like this. I didn't like Mr. Porter much, but maybe he didn't like his life much. No family of his own, just borrowing his sister's. She had called to tell him about the tournament, but she hadn't invited him along. Instead he had to read the details in the newspaper.

"I just don't want that stuff in my refrigerator." His voice was flat, not angry.

I had to say it: "It's a school project."

"I know. And I'll get the flour for you. By Thursday." He turned to the sink and dumped out his coffee. He ran water over a washrag, wrung it out, and started wiping down the cabinet tops. "Get your shoes. We leave in five minutes."

For once, I was grateful my school shoes were too large: I wouldn't have to ask him about new shoes for a long time. But maybe today, we had made some progress.

BREAD PROJECT: WEEK 2

ELIOT

Friday morning, I was sitting at the counter eating toast when Marj came in.

"Look at this," she wailed. She spread her fingers and showed me the new blisters that had popped up overnight.

I had itched a day or two, then it dried up. Hers kept getting worse.

"Between the fingers is the worst," she said. "Itches like crazy."

I cringed and tried not to think about germs and get that going again.

"I'll have to get a shot today. That's what Dr. Jamieson said on Tuesday; if it didn't get better, I'd have to have a shot." Marj's freckled face was flushed. Looked almost hysterical.

A quiet despair shot through me, and I shoved away the cereal bowl. I had only mown the grass. Only trimmed the shrubs. Only tried to help.

Marj was dressed for work, wearing a business suit.

I squirmed, awkward, wondering what to say. "You could stay home."

She shrugged and blew on her hands, as if that would stop the itching. Then, she looked up, startled. "What's today?"

"Friday."

"The Bread Project. I can't do the assembly."

The despair? It deepened. I clenched my jaw, trying to keep my emotions under control. Nothing could be allowed to stop the Bread Project, or I would have to go to a foster family right away. But I had undermined it myself with that poison ivy. "Maybe Mrs. Lopez could do the assembly today?"

The wrinkle between Marj's eyebrows cleared. "Of course. We do have friends."

She went to her office, and I heard her muffled voice.

A few minutes later, she came back barefoot and calmer. "Mrs. Lopez and I decided to cancel the assembly today. I had the sack of names, so I drew one out. Sameer Patel will get the sourdough, but Mr. Benton will call him in to let him know. Alli can give it to him at the end of school. I have a doctor's visit in an hour, then I will come home and take a nap." She abruptly stopped talking.

Relieved that her day would be easy, I picked up my bowl and dumped the soggy cereal into the sink, then put it into the dishwasher. When I looked up, Marj was looking at me.

I stopped moving, suddenly worried.

She spoke quietly. "When I wake up, I'll be cleaning the house. A real estate agent is coming by tomorrow. Just to walk through and tell me what repair work needs to be done to sell the house. Not listing it for sale yet. Just wanted you know."

Nice to be warned. "Thanks."

When I woke early Saturday, there was just one thought: realtor coming. It was a solid reminder of Marj's intentions to send me to the experts in raising boys. I wanted to fight against it, but how? To fight it, I needed to support everything Marj did and make it easy for her to raise a son. That meant, in spite of my foul mood, I needed to mow the lawn, without her even asking.

Dressed in old jeans and tennis shoes, I went out to the garage. It was neat, orderly, Griff's garage. All the tools were on pegboards. Each tool was outlined in black, so you knew where to put it back. So you could find it next time, Griff said.

If Marj moved, would she let me keep the tools? I'd really like that. I remember Griff holding the wooden handles, his thumb rubbing the polished wood. He especially loved the old wooden plane, the one he had from his grandfather.

I let the ache for Griff wash through me. But I knew better than to let memory take over, or I wouldn't get the lawn mown.

I heaved the push mower onto the workbench and studied the dull, dirty blades. First, I'd have to sharpen the blades. I wiped each blade with a paper towel, and then used one of Griff's metal files to smooth a few rough spots. Lastly I picked up the grinding paste. Didn't know if I'd remember everything right, but I had to try.

Unscrewing the lid, I dipped a brush into the goop and painted it on the last half inch of each blade. Next, I inserted the handle and cranked backwards. It made the mower's frame into a sort of grinding stone.

Didn't take long for my muscles to protest. But I liked the rhythmic noise; it drowned out everything. No thinking, no feeling. Just doing. Grateful for the distraction, I zoned out.

"Hello!"

"Wha–" I dropped the crank and spun around. It was the school nurse, standing in the garage door. "Miss Clay?"

"Oh. You're Eliot, is that right?"

"Yes."

"I'm looking for Mrs. Winston. I'm here to look at the house and yard."

"What?"

"Oh." Her eyes twinkled. "You're confused. Well, by day, I'm the school nurse. By night, I'm a real estate agent, a realtor."

"Oh. The realtor." I did remember her saying something about real estate. You just never expect to see teachers outside school. She wore the same khaki pants as at school, but a nicer top and a nametag from the realty company. Suddenly, I worried. "I, uh, haven't got the yard mowed yet this morning."

She waved a hand. "It's okay. I can tell you're doing a good job. When we get ready to show it, you'll have it ready. Right?"

"Yes, ma'am. I will."

"Um, Mrs. Winston. Is she home?"

I flushed, embarrassed to realize I was staring. I wiped the grinding goop on my shorts and said, "Yes, Ma'am, she's home." Then, I shivered. Goop covered my hands. Germy goop.

Quickly, I led Miss Clay inside. The breakfast nook was bathed in golden light. Marj sat hunched over, warming a coffee mug with her hands, her fingers pale, fragile. The shot for the poison ivy was already working, and her hands were not as swollen, not as red. On the table lay a crumpled bag of pretzels, probably all she ate for breakfast. She was staring out the window, her face a vacant mask.

When she saw Miss Clay, Marj set down the coffee and yawned. "Sorry. I'm starting slowly this morning."

Miss Clay nodded. Almost yawned herself. "Worst part of a realtor's job, getting up too early on Saturdays." She smiled at me. "Eliot was working early, too, fixing the lawn mower. I told him the yard looked great, so not to worry about it for me today."

Marj leaned her head to one side and smiled at me, too. "Thanks, Eliot."

I pulled my germy hands behind my back and nodded, grateful that Miss Clay had pointed out my hard work.

Marj motioned for Miss Clay to sit down.

While they chatted, I went to the kitchen sink and squirted liquid soap on my hands and scrubbed. Scrubbed hard.

By the time I finished, Marj and Miss Clay were strolling around, Marj carrying a notebook and pen. I followed, proud of this house, wanting to watch Miss Clay be impressed by the Winston family home.

But Marj explained and excused: The fireplace hadn't been used in over ten years, but it just needed the chimney cleaned, she said. Eliot replaced the doorstop in the hallway for me, but I haven't had time yet to fix the dented wall. Yes, the arched doorways between the living room and dining room were original. Yes, there were tiny bits of old wallpaper still stuck near the ceiling, but they should be easy to remove.

Just like Griff, Miss Clay smelled like a school nurse, half Pine-Sol and half rubbing alcohol. On Miss Clay, though, the smell was wrong. Wrong, like letting Miss Clay look around our house was wrong.

"That rug looks worn," Miss Clay said, pointing to the runner that stretched up the stairs. "You'll have to replace it."

Outraged, I started to say the rug was soft and easy on bare feet. But I looked again. And saw a couple of bare patches. My face flushed and I was suddenly hot, embarrassed.

Marj jotted another note, adding it to the list of details that needed to be taken care of before the house might sell. She waved at me to lead the way upstairs.

So up I went, worried now about how old the carpet was in my room. Coming out of the stairwell, the room opened up and covered the whole second floor. Not that it was huge, it just covered the center part of the house. I always thought of it as the cockpit of a flying saucer. It was sunny and hot in the summer and sunny and cold in the winter. I had loved this room from the moment I saw it.

Miss Clay had lots to say, though. "Of course, replace this carpet. And that dirty sneaker smell has to go. Get some plug-in room deodorizers."

Miss Clay had been unsure of herself at school, but as a realtor, she didn't mind giving her opinion. She wanted the broken rack in the closet fixed, the ceiling fan dusted, the walls painted. "And try to hire a window cleaner before you put up new curtains."

Finished upstairs, Miss Clay led the way downstairs. "I think," she said, "my client will love this house when you do the few clean-ups and fix-ups."

Few? I wanted to fume at her for giving Marj such a long list.

Miss Clay shrugged. "But he has one more requirement. It's strange. He wants me to measure the useable space in the attic. His wife has tons of Christmas ornaments–she goes overboard at holidays–and he wants plenty of space to store that stuff."

Marj nodded, absently. She was studying the note pad with an accountant's eye, adding up how much the repairs and new paint and carpet would cost. Too much. I could tell her that.

"Eliot, will you show Miss Clay the attic?"

I obeyed, reluctantly, "This way."

Back in the garage, I jumped to reach the rope of the pull-down door.

Miss Clay reached up and helped unfold the steps, then shook her head, her ponytail swinging. "Broken step here. Remind me to tell your mom." She stopped to look around. "But the garage is really clean."

Of course. It was Griff's garage.

When I stepped onto the stairway, a loud creak made me stop. Were the hinges okay? Griff never went into the attic that I knew of. When the creak didn't repeat, I climbed, eager now to see what was up there.

Poking my head into the attic space, I coughed. And words rattled around my head. Dusty, musty, crusty, rusty. The attic was dark, almost scary. But curiosity won. Marj had said there was a pull chain light just to the right of the opening. I stepped onto a rough wood flooring and waved around until a string brushed my hand.

Grabbing the string, I pulled, setting the hanging light to swinging. A pale light washed back and forth.

Unpainted, aged wood–brittle and dark–stretched into the shadows where the roofline lowered to meet the walls. Right around my feet, plywood flooring created a storage area. Past that? Cotton-like stuff covered with an inch of dust, at least. Insulation, but old insulation.

Miss Clay stood beside me now, and we looked all around.

Toward the rear of the storage area were some cardboard boxes. And two plastic clothing bags: inside were uniforms, maybe military uniforms, with buttons and sewn-on badges and things. I hadn't known that Griff was in the military, had no idea if it was Army or Navy or whatever. Maybe they were from some uncle or cousin or grandfather. Curious, I unzipped the bag, but jerked back.

Mothballs! The smell overwhelmed me.

I sneezed.

And then, I shivered. And then, it started.

I couldn't breathe. Germs, millions of germs.

"It's too dirty up here," Miss Clay complained. "Let's get it measured and get out." She handed me the end of a tape measure and motioned for me to hold it at the far side. She walked away, pulling the tape out to stretch along the floored area.

I bent over. Held the tape at the edge of the plywood. I swayed. Dizzy.

My skin was itchy, cringey. My hand was just inches away from the cottony insulation.

I bit my lip. Fought to keep control. Now, my heart was pounding, pounding, pounding. Dizzy. About to lose control. About to freak out, right in front of the school nurse.

"Got that one. Do the other side," Miss Clay said.

Her calm, relaxed voice helped me get a grip on the panic.

I stumbled over the cardboard boxes, sending up a shower of dust. "Sorry," I mumbled. I shoved the papers and books back into the box. It looked like school yearbooks, maybe Griff's.

"That's right, just hold it over there." Miss Clay said.

I barely heard her; the dust settling on me again, the light still swinging and casting long shifting shadows. I bent. Then collapsed. Sat in an awkward cross-legged heap. Somehow, I held the tape in the right place. And fought to keep control. I wanted to leap into a swimming pool and dunk under and get rid of the crawly stuff on my hands, my arms, my legs.

"That's it. Let's go."

The tape measure retracted with a thunk.

I rushed for the square of daylight. Get me out of here. Right now.

Gritted my teeth. Took two steps down. Shaking too much to put all my weight on my legs, I leaned forward and held onto the attic floor and closed my eyes. The shaking stopped and I half-slid, half-fell down the rest of the steps.

In the open garage doorway, away from the attic, I slapped dust from my clothes and gulped fresh air in relief. But the dust covered me, like a cloud of worry. I sneezed.

Again, a big, loud sneeze.

Then, I started coughing and couldn't stop.

"You must be allergic to something up there."

I closed my eyes and gasped. No. Deep, slow breaths, I told myself. This wasn't real. No need to panic. When my breath was more regular, I opened my eyes.

Miss Clay stood right in front of me with her eyes narrowed. "Or is it something else?"

I took my time. Deep, slow breaths. "No." Breathe. "It's just dust." Breathe.

"I don't think so."

"Yes, dust. Or allergies." I spoke slowly, trying to sound confident. "That's all."

"Maybe I should talk to your mom–"

"No." It was louder than I meant. "No," I said quieter. "She's still so upset after my Dad–After he–. Well, since he's been gone."

She nodded; so she'd heard our story somewhere and understood what I was talking about. But she wasn't totally convinced. "Have you ever done this before?"

"Done what?"

"Run out of a room? Been sort of panicky?"

"That attic was too dirty. You said it yourself."

"But have you done this before?"

Miss Clay tried to put her fingers on my wrist. Tried to take my pulse!

I pulled away. If Marj found out–I was sure Griff had never told her–it would be just one more reason to send me away.

"No, I've never done that before." I relaxed my face muscles. I lifted my shoulders and let them fall in a casual shrug.

"Okay. I turned off the light and closed the stairs," Miss Clay said. "And I got the measurements. I'll just say good-bye to Mrs. Winston and let you have your Saturday back." She disappeared into the house.

Shaking now from relief, I stumbled to the workbench and collapsed. By the time Miss Clay passed me a few minutes later, I was sharpening the blades of the push mower again. Cranking hard. Trying to zone out again.

ALLI

Walking into the garage of Eliot's house, I stopped and sniffed. A sort of waxy smell, and maybe oil. Bent over, Eliot didn't see me at first. He was working on an old-fashioned lawn mower, one without a motor. His face was shadowed. "What are you doing?" I asked.

"Sharpening the blades." Now, he looked up and grinned, and I guess I had just imagined the shadows. "What's up?"

"I'm worried about the Bread Project."

"Why?"

"Sam Patel."

"He should be okay."

"No." I sat on the floor where I could watch Eliot work. Looked like he was cleaning some gunk off each blade. Carefully, because they looked sharp. While he worked, I explained how I'd given Sam his jar of sourdough starter yesterday after school. "Outside Mr. Benton's office, though, Sam stopped to talk to a friend. Said he wasn't going to tell his Mom about the project. He shut up when he saw me, but I heard enough. We've got to check up on him. Make sure his parents understand how important this project is for the school."

Taking care of the sourdough all week– feeding it, checking daily to see how it grew, smelling it–it was better than the pet rocks that Mandy told me about when she was in junior high. I had liked the project because of Mrs. Winston's kindness. Now, I liked the project 'cause it was fun.

"Are you for real?" Eliot said. "You want to call his parents? That's really pushing hard."

"Isn't that what you want me to do?"

"Yeah, but, well, I'd never call a parent. Too embarrassing."

"Let's get a sandwich," I suggested. "We can talk while we eat."

Eliot held a rag over the lawn mower blade and stared at me.

"What?" I said. "You asked for my help, remember?"

He threw the rag onto the workbench, swung his leg over and stood. "I'll fix you lunch. But you don't have to visit the Patels to earn it."

"Hey, if I'm helping, we're doing it right. We'll check up on Sam. Oh, I'll eat, 'cause you owe me. But then we're going to visit the Patels."

Eliot rolled his eyes. "Uh. No. We're not."

Following him into the kitchen, I said to his back, "Uh. Yes. I already called Mrs. Patel. She expects us. Both of us. In an hour."

Eliot slapped peanut butter onto bread, then held a banana above the peanut butter and hacked away. Thick slices landed where they would. He slapped another piece of bread on top, handed it to me and started on his own sandwich.

I opened the sandwich and stared. "This is exactly why we have to go over there. I've never seen anyone make peanut butter and banana sandwiches like that. You're supposed to smash the bananas and mix it with the peanut butter."

"I bet the Patels have never even baked a loaf of bread," Eliot said.

"Because they are from India?" I said. "Sam was born here, you know, that's what Mrs. Patel said. He's a US citizen."

"You got that chatty with her?" Eliot's eyes were huge.

"I just talked a few minutes. Unlike you, some people don't mind telling about their lives."

"Crazy to ask and crazy for her to tell." Eliot shrugged, then took a bite of his sandwich.

"Well, we're still going over there to talk about the project. I didn't get to explain it all on the phone."

For the next few minutes, we just ate. Then I made up two more peanut butter and banana sandwiches, this time with smashed up bananas. We ate those and compared the difference in taste.

"Mine's better," Eliot said.

I had planned his afternoon for him. And I was forcing him to go to the Patels. So, I let him win this one. "I do like your recipe better."

He sighed. "How are we getting to the Patels?"

Eliot would never think to check up on Sam, but without this kind of attention, the project would fail. We just had to find out if

Mrs. Patel understood what Sam had to do for the project. We didn't have to stay long.

I grinned. "You've got two bikes in the garage."

ELIOT

After telling Marj that we were going to the Patels, I wheeled my bike out of the garage. Alli jumped on my old bike, and we pedaled away toward the Southside Apartments. The red brick apartment complex was a Zane property. Neat, clean, even prosperous looking. We locked the bikes to a stairway and climbed up to 11-J.

Alli bounded ahead and knocked on the apartment door.

Sam opened the door. "Hello."

He wore his earpiece in one ear. And like Alli, he wore his school uniform, khaki shorts and school shirt. His surprise was evident.

And now, I was embarrassed. I played on a soccer team with him a couple times. He played goalie, while I played offense. But otherwise, we had barely talked. Now, we were on his doorstep. "Look, we just–"

But from inside, a woman's voice called, "That's probably your friends. They called early this morning to say they were coming. Tell them to come in."

Sam's dark eyes flashed. "Mother says you must come in and visit."

Angry, I pushed past Alli. I said low, so just Alli could hear, "Your friends. You told Mrs. Patel that we were Sam's friends?"

She just tossed her head.

Inside, Sam stopped at a small rug with shoes lined up on it. "We take our shoes off inside. If you please."

I slipped off my tennis shoes, but winced. Smelly socks.

Looking around the apartment, the first thing I noticed was the smell of bread baking. And it smelled like sourdough bread.

The second thing I noticed was that the apartment looked like a regular American apartment. Well, what had I expected? Bright fabrics, marble floors, strange music, lidded baskets with cobras? Well, something exotic and, well, Indian. Instead there was a big screen TV with a game system, a large fish tank with colorful fish, and comfortable-looking couches and chairs.

Mrs. Patel entered the room, and immediately you had to turn and watch her. Here was the foreign stuff I had expected: her sari was bright turquoise, and when she walked, her bracelets sounded, clink, clink, clink. After introductions, she turned to Sam. "Now, what is this about the sourdough starter? Alli says it is a school project."

Before Sam could answer, Alli launched into an explanation, complete with large hand gestures and lots of repetition. I squirmed, listening to her chatter on and on. She could have said it much faster and shorter.

Finally, I interrupted. "We didn't want to bother you, Mrs. Patel. It's just an unusual project, and we're just making sure everyone understands it."

Mrs. Patel motioned for Sam to sit beside her. When he moved to her side, she hugged him. He grimaced.

"No, Sameer didn't understand," Mrs. Patel said. "I've used sourdough starter before, of course, but didn't know this was a school assignment. I just thought someone was being nice and passing out starter, so I baked bread today and used it all."

"All of it?" This didn't sound good.

"Yes, I'm sorry."

From the kitchen, a timer started to ding, ding, ding. "Excuse me, I'll be right back," Mrs. Patel said.

As soon as she was gone, Sam whispered, "Why'd you have to ruin everything? I didn't want to take care of that stuff for weeks and weeks. If I had walked home yesterday, I would have dumped it. But Mother picked me up."

"But you have to take care of it," Alli said. "Or, the Bread Project will fail."

"And that's bad because?" Sam said.

Mrs. Patel returned and held out a plate with a large bread-like thing–still hot, with steam rising. I took a deep whiff. It was sourdough, but it was an irregular circle that covered the whole plate, so that I couldn't figure out how it was cooked. It smelled so good.

At my hungry look, Mrs. Patel smiled. "With the sourdough starter, I made naan, like my mother's mother always did. I haven't made *naan* in so long, and my husband was so pleased that I made extra."

"It's not a loaf of bread," I said. Then felt stupid. But Mrs. Patel was nice about it.

"No, it's a flat bread from northern India. Would you like some? I'll leave this one here for the three of you to eat."

Eagerly, Alli and I broke off pieces of the *naan* and ate.

"Heavenly," I said, using Griff's word again. And Alli nodded.

Apparently, Sam wasn't impressed with the *naan*. While we ate, he turned on his game system and played. Just when I was thinking it was time to go, he handed me the controller. Then Alli took a turn. We repeated the cycle, and by then, we were cheering for each other.

"Next level, all right!"

It was fun.

After a while, Mrs. Patel appeared with a tray of glasses and set them down on the table for us. Smoothies. I was taking my turn, so I didn't taste mine yet.

Alli asked, "What flavor is this?"

"Mango yogurt," Sam said.

"Heavenly," she said.

When I finally handed off the controller and tasted my smoothie, I agreed.

I was surprised when Sam turned on a lamp. Looking around, it was getting late, almost sunset. Surprised, I rose, stretched and said, "We'd better go. We'll bring you more starter tomorrow." It had been a fast afternoon.

"Look, this was fun," Sam waved at the game and the empty smoothie glasses. "I'm glad you came over. But do you have to bring more sourdough stuff?"

I felt for him. But I needed the Bread Project so I could have time to get through to Marj. Besides, Alli had already called for Mrs. Patel.

She stepped out of the kitchen and said, "Yes?"

The turquoise sari startled me again with its foreignness. The apartment smelled spicy now, too. Curry, I thought, though I didn't know where I got that word. Never eaten curry. But after that *naan* and the mango smoothie, I bet it was good.

"We'll bring you more sourdough starter tomorrow," Alli said. "Mine has to grow a week, but Eliot can take some out of his jar."

"Great. So, as long as Sam keeps it alive and has enough to share each Friday, we can cook with it?"

"Yes," Alli said.

"And his grade is based just on bringing in starter each Friday?"

I nodded. No teacher had actually said they would take off points for not bringing back starter the next week, but I figured it was the right thing to tell Mrs. Patel.

"I'll make sure he keeps that grade up," she said.

I sighed in relief. And decided that Sam was okay. Next time I got to choose sides for soccer, I'd pick him right after Toby.

"Thank you," Alli said. "And, if you don't mind, could I have the recipe for *naan*?"

Mrs. Patel beamed. "Yes. Thanks for asking." She pulled an index card from the hall desk and rummaged in a drawer for a pencil. Then she stopped. "Why not collect bread recipes from other families, too? We could sell a Bread Project Cookbook as an additional fund raiser." Her dark eyes were shining.

Alli's smile turned to a grimace. "That sounds like lots of work."

"Oh, no. We mothers could do it. I'd just put it into a database. It would be easy."

I lifted an eyebrow. She didn't look like a computer genius. Not with that sari and bracelets.

Sam pointed to a computer workstation in the corner. "Mother is a computer programmer. She does things like that." He shrugged. "She'll probably find some place to upload the recipes and get it printed out, too. For a good price. She does that."

Mrs. Patel smiled, white teeth flashing in her brown face. "Sameer is right. It sounds like a good project for me. Sometimes, I feel like–" She stopped.

"Like what?" I asked.

Mrs. Patel flapped her hand a couple times. "Oh, nothing. It's just that, well, sometimes, you know, I don't feel like we're a real part of the school community. I'd just like to help."

"More help would be great," I said. "I'll tell Mrs. Lopez and Marj about the cookbook idea, and they'll call you later."

Leaving, Alli stomped down the steps and jerked her bike away as soon as the lock was off.

"What?" I demanded.

"It makes me mad. The Patels don't feel like their family is part of the school. It's wrong, that's what."

It was something Griff would have said. The Bread Project wouldn't have been a chore for Griff, but a semester-long excuse to visit people. To enjoy listening to each family's story. To taste their bread recipes. Because I lived with Griff for two years, I understood. But without Griff here, it was hard to do by myself.

"Thanks for making us go over there," I said. "It was the right thing to do."

Alli grinned at me. "By the way, the Porters are going out for dinner with friends. What's for supper?"

BREAD PROJECT:

WEEKS 3, 4, 5, 6

ELIOT

After that rough start, the fall season fell into a pattern. On Fridays, the sourdough starter passed to new students, and on Friday night, Alli called the newest family and set up a time that weekend to explain the project. We tasted a wide variety of breads: *pitas* at the Zanes, who had a Greek heritage, *ekmek* at the Vasins, who were Turkish immigrants, *ciabatta* from the Donatellis, who had Italian heritage. I was amazed at how my family's humble sourdough starter adapted so easily for each family.

Mrs. Patel enlisted the help of Mrs. Johnson and Mrs. Lopez to talk to parents and gather recipes and stories for the cookbook. Each week was a little easier as the word spread. With so many countries represented, it should be a great cookbook, they all said.

1 - 2 - 4 - 8 - 16. By the time the sourdough starter passed to 32 students, though, things were getting more difficult. Altogether (1 + 2 + 4 + 8 + 16 + 32=63), 63 students would have the sourdough. The next week, right before Halloween, 63 more would receive their jars and we would finally be giving starter to some fifth graders.

After that, it would go so rapidly that there was no way we could visit every family. Would the project fall apart at that point? Alli and I worried about what to do, but could think of nothing.

Meanwhile, to add to the chaos of the Bread Project, about mid-October our house was turned into an obstacle course. Ladders. Paint drop cloths. Ripped up carpet. Marj had hired Mr. and Mrs. Johnson–Kinesha's parents–to paint, paper and do repairs. Saw horses rode the range in Griff's garage. Fat electrical cords slithered around the concrete floor to the power tools.

By the end of October, most of the repair work and papering was done, and only painting was left. One afternoon, I came in from school and found Mrs. Johnson in the breakfast room, looking at paint samples.

When she saw me, she said, "Your mom just called. She's hung up in road construction and will be a few minutes late."

Marj had been complaining there were torn-up roads on her way to the office, too many to avoid by using back streets. She had been leaving early in the mornings to get to work on time. "Thanks for telling me," I said.

Mrs. Johnson nodded, then pulled out paint chips in a range of deep shades.

"What color do you want for your room?" she asked.

I plopped my backpack on a chair and leaned over the table. I ran a finger across a section of the samples. "I like these."

"Ah, the jewel tones. They would look good in this house," she agreed.

I studied the colors, pushing them in or out, trying to imagine my sunny room with one of these deep colors. At first I had hated all the work being done, but as it progressed, I realized the house had needed a lot of fixing up. It was looking better all the time. And it pleased me that I could choose my own colors, and I wanted to be careful to get it right. Finally, I pulled out a dark green, "forest glen." I held it up and said, "This one?"

Just then, Marj stepped into the room. "Sorry I'm late."

"We were just looking at colors," Mrs. Johnson said pleasantly.

Marj picked up the strips and pushed the dark colors back into the stack and pulled out the strips of pale colors, mostly whites. "Miss Clay says that plain white walls make a house easier to sell."

Mrs. Johnson raised her eyebrow at me, but I just leaned back in my chair and watched Marj push around the shades of white.

Leaves had been dropping rapidly from our trees, and the tree cover no longer protected this room from the afternoon sun. So when the sun sank a bit lower, a shaft of light stabbed directly into my eyes. I was getting so tired of hearing what Miss Clay thought would sell. I shoved away from the table and grabbed my backpack. "I'm going upstairs," I said.

Behind me, I heard Mrs. Johnson agree with Marj and Miss Clay. "White does sell better, if that's your goal. These five whites are the most popular. Kinda boring, though," she said.

"But safe," said Marj firmly.

I clomped up the stairs and sat on the bed looking around, trying to imagine the already bright room getting even brighter when painted white.

Shaking my head, I went downstairs again to check the crock-pot. We had gotten better about planning ahead and often did a crock-pot recipe once a week and ate leftovers for several days. Today, it was a roast, and the smell made me hungry. Marj and Mrs. Johnson came out of the breakfast room smiling.

"Vanilla White, it is," Mrs. Johnson said. "Now. We prefer oil paint. It lasts longer and looks better."

Marj nodded, "Fine."

"Good." Mrs. Johnson said. "We'll order paint tonight and get started tomorrow. Should be just a couple more days to get this job wrapped up." She waved, then walked down the hallway to the garage, where Mr. Johnson was waiting.

Marj perched on a kitchen stool and started punching numbers into a calculator.

I was surprised at how sad I suddenly felt, thinking about the breakfast room white instead of its cheery yellow. "Will the oil paint cost more?"

Marj looked up startled. "I got a big check from Griff's life insurance last week. I can afford it now."

"Oh." Questions crowded my mind. How much? Would Marj stop worrying about money now? And then my stomach churned. This was so wrong. Thinking about how much money we got because Griff was gone.

"I'd rather have Griff back than any amount of money. But he made sure I wouldn't have any money worries. He always put others first."

I nodded, knowing she was right. Yet, still wishing for the impossible. And I still felt guilty for wanting to know how much the insurance had paid.

Marj half stood, like she might come over and hug me. But she sank back onto her stool. "Since Griff adopted you, you're his son, half the money is yours."

Stunned, I just shook my head.

She went on, "I'm putting it in a trust for you. You'll get it when you're 21."

I had never thought about getting part of the money for myself. No, I couldn't take it. I would feel guilty using it, even for an allowance.

Putting down her calculator, Marj said, "Don't worry. My half of the money is more than enough; we can afford to get all this work done."

I hesitated. But I had to say it. "Tomorrow is Halloween."

"Yes," Marj said. She started setting out plates, glasses, silverware. "Remember, we have to work at the Community Center's Harvest Party. The Bread Project has that booth, and we'll have bread samples and recipes to pass out."

"Oh, yeah." I remembered all right.

Last month, the PTA women had met at our house to talk about the project and how to let more people know about it.

"School and community center, they're the two places Griff took me all the time," I told them.

So Mrs. Patel called the community center and found out there were still some open booths at the Halloween party. In southern Nashville, the community center had a tradition of doing the Halloween Carnival, so none of the elementary schools did one. Instead, they encouraged families to attend the community center.

"Maybe we'll pick up some sponsors there," Mrs. Lopez said.

Now, as I made salads, breaking apart lettuce leaves into a bowl and adding cherry tomatoes, I worked up courage to ask, "Can I trick-or-treat afterwards with Toby and Alli and some of the other kids?"

Marj's freckled face grimaced. "I never liked this holiday much. When I was little, the masks scared me, and when I was older, they made me uncomfortable. Too sweaty, and you can't see anything." She shivered.

"I love the masks. We just want to trick or treat for a few minutes? We'll just go a few places in the neighborhood."

"Depends on how long the party lasts at the Community Center." She poured milk into my glass and iced tea into hers.

"Okay." I felt stabbed in the chest. Next year, in junior high, that was too old for trick-or-treating. This was my last chance. Desperate, I asked, "What about a costume for the Community Center party?"

"Oh." Marj gave me a blank look. Ran a hand through her hair. It had grown out and was no longer a precision cut. Instead, she looked like she was a scarecrow for Halloween. As soon as I thought that, I tried to get rid of the idea because her hair was softer than straw. Of course. But it did stick out funny.

"Well," Marj said, "Can't you find some dress-up thing here at the house? I don't want to go out and buy something that you'll only wear one night."

"But it's Halloween."

Marj made a clicking sound with her tongue, like a staccato drum beat. "Check the attic. There are boxes of stuff up there."

"Yeah, I'll do that." I tried not to care, just sat and ate salad and roast and baked potatoes and barely tasted it. My heart was in my boots. No super-hero costume for me. Just mothballs and dust and germs.

No, I couldn't go up into the attic again.

But Marj wasn't going to spend anything on a costume, and I needed something for tomorrow night. For a treacherous moment, I wondered again about the insurance payment and how much it was. But that didn't matter. Making it till Thanksgiving was the only thing that mattered. It mattered even more than a Halloween costume.

After I helped clean the kitchen and Marj had disappeared into her office to make some calls, I reluctantly went to the garage and pulled down the attic steps. Miss Clay had forgotten to tell Marj about the broken step. At least one thing had escaped Miss Clay, I thought in satisfaction.

Standing there at the bottom, I was full of dread. Yet, in an odd way, this was good, to test myself when no one else was around. Step by step, I climbed and pulled out onto the plywood floor.

The attic smelled hot. Hot wasn't supposed to be a smell, but that was the best description. Yes, it smelled like old wood and inches of dust and musty old things. But it also smelled hot. Like the inside of an oven might smell if you subtracted the bread smell. Surprisingly, though, I didn't feel panicky. Not yet, anyway.

I pulled the light chain and walked straight to the clothes bags, my best chance for a costume. Kept my eyes straight ahead. No looking around at things that might start a panic. I unzipped the bag, holding my breath against the mothball smell.

There were two wool military uniforms. Marines from World War II. Or at least that's what it looked like to me. And an Army uniform from World War I. Both were too big, too hot to wear. I zipped the bag up.

And started feeling itchy.

Best to go down now. Look for a costume downstairs. Or go without a costume.

I stopped to pull a couple school yearbooks from the old cardboard box. I'd take them to my room and read them later.

Downstairs, standing in the open garage door, I smiled at the last touches of sunset, the orange and purple swirling in the clouds. I was out of the hot smell. And this time, I hadn't gotten panicky. I was getting better, able to control it. Maybe this, at least, was looking up.

ALLI

That fall, the weeks just flew by. I was still uncomfortable at the Porters. Only difference–now it was a familiar uncomfortable. Livable, I guess. Same thing at the Wilma Rudolph Elementary School. Grades were good, I never had to worry about that. And I knew more people. Still missed my old school, though.

For sticking it out here, I felt I deserved a guerdon. (Guerdon: Middle English derivation. Definition: A reward. G-u-e-r-d-o-n. Winning word in the 2008 spelling bee.)

Each Sunday afternoon that fall, I used the Porter's computer or Eliot's computer and read the BabyPayne.com blog. Each week, I held my breath until I read that everything with Mandy and Baby was still okay. Mimi had gone home until Baby came, and Mandy was working part time again.

Ted wrote a lot: I loved the weekly reports and the reports on the doctor's visits. How much the doctor guessed the baby weighed now. The pink quilts that Mandy had bought that week–Ted even posted a picture. Things like that.

Baby was due about a week before Thanksgiving. After reading the blog updates, I studied online about babies growing inside a mama and figured Mandy's baby was doing just fine. I wanted to see the ultrasound pictures, and finally Ted posted one. You could even see Baby's profile, her tiny nose.

So, my determination grew: I would go to the hospital to see Baby. Lay my eyes on Baby for myself and know that I hadn't caused any problems with that accident.

The early fall passed. Thinking about Baby or visiting families for the Bread Project or doing homework. And then, it was Halloween.

Mandy and Ted didn't care much for Halloween. Oh, we went to carnivals at school, or did some trick-or-treating. But no enthusiasm.

This year–it would be different. The Community Center started passing out brochures for its annual carnival, and it looked like fun. For one thing, several schools in the area attended, and there would be more people, lots of excitement.

Really, what I love about Halloween is the masks. Something about hiding your face; it's great. It makes me into somebody else.

After school on the 31st, I asked Mr. Porter if I could walk home. I took some of the money I won from Toby, stopped by a store and bought a two masks, one for me and one for Eliot, who said Marj didn't do anything about a costume for him. I didn't want a costume, nothing fancy. Just a facemask was enough. The kind that make you look like a raccoon.

Then I skipped back to Mr. Porter's, whistling.

Opening the front door, I heard Mr. Porter whistling, too. Funny, guess I had taken up his habit. Went through the living room to the kitchen, where the table was spread with three large bowls, and Mr. Porter was dumping bags of candy into each one. Then stirring up the mix with both hands.

I set my shopping bag on a chair and knelt on another chair. "Can I help?"

Mr. Porter shook his head no.

He finished dumping out the candy, then smiled. Motioned for me to take something.

No need to ask me twice. I took a tiny bag of candy corn. My favorite.

"You'll think this strange, but I love giving out candy, and the kids around here know it," he said. "I'll dress up in a costume and be here for hours." Somehow, the holiday put him in a talkative mood. "My dad loved Halloween. You know, my sister and I always dressed up as a pair. Cowboy and cowgirl. Space astronauts. My parents loved to hold parties and decorate and—" He trailed off.

His ugly face looked almost kind. He had his routines, his ways of doing things and obviously loved this holiday like none other. Strange, but I guess everyone has some soft spot.

I thought I should reassure him, let him know that I was taken care of for tonight. "Eliot said he and Mrs. Winston would come by and pick me up. We'll go to the Community Center and then trick-or-treat for a while."

I ripped open the candy corn package and bit off the white end of one piece and smiled up at Mr. Porter.

But he was frowning. "I tried the Community Center party the first year or two they did it. But, it was boring for me. I like passing out candy here."

"Sounds like you had nice parents." I struggled to figure out what to say. "Sounds like they started nice traditions for Halloween."

"Mom and Dad were great." Idly, he stirred the candy around again. "I'm trying to be a good parent, just like they were. That's why I need to talk to you," he said, "about Eliot. And Toby."

"Yes?" I ate the tip from the next candy corn, then the middle and then the last section.

"Miss Clay says she has seen you playing cards with those boys."

I shrugged. "Yes."

"She says you play for money."

"Sometimes."

"You gamble? You're playing cards and gambling? You admit this?"

"It's just for fun. It's not a lot of money." Besides, I thought, we only played once a week or so, anyway.

Mr. Porter stood and paced, two steps to the fancy stove that rarely got used, then five steps back to the wall with the fridge and the microwave. The freezer was full of frozen dinners now–he'd gotten in the habit of Friday night grocery shopping–so I had become an expert at microwaving stuff.

"Alli, I'm going to have to ask you to stop gambling with Toby and Eliot."

I was totally surprised. I turned in my chair to watch him, still pacing. "Why?"

"Because, well, because I said so, and I've asked you not to do it."

I shook my head, trying to understand. What had Mr. Porter so riled up? Just a card game? "I don't–"

But Mr. Porter interrupted. "I don't care if you think it's silly. Or if you think the amount you gamble isn't enough to worry about. Growing up, we were taught that gambling was a sin. Now, I don't go that far, but in grade school, my best friend's mother, old Mrs. Pardo–" he broke off and stood with his arms crossed. "I don't have to explain it to you. You're a guest in my house, and I won't stand for a gambler living here."

I closed my mouth and crossed my arms. "Then give me an allowance."

Mr. Porter stepped backward, his eyes wide and shocked, like I had slapped him. "Allowance? Why?"

"So I can buy the things I need."

He took two quick steps to the table, snatched up my shopping bag and pulled out the masks. "Like this?" He threw them onto the table. "You need masks? Two of them?"

"One for me, one for Eliot."

"And Eliot can't buy his own?"

By now, I knew about Eliot's dad up-and-dying, and about Marj being unsure-about-adoption. I couldn't answer that question without telling Mr. Porter more about Eliot's life than Eliot would like. "I just wanted to give him one."

"You're sweet on him?"

Now, I blushed. "NO! It's not that."

Mr. Porter stepped back again and waved his hands, cutting off anything else I might say. "Doesn't matter. No more gambling. Do you hear? I'd like it even better if you'd find different friends. But for sure, no cards, no gambling."

Great. Where would I get money now? There were just things that kids needed. Like the almost-empty jar of peanut butter in my desk drawer upstairs. Mr. Porter wouldn't even buy peanut butter for me. Sure, he was doing better at getting food, but only food he approved of. Okay. Fair enough. His money, his choice. But my money, my choice. I wanted peanut butter and I would need another jar of it soon.

I stood, trying to stretch my backbone to be taller than Mr. Porter. Keeping my face calm, I picked up the masks. The bowls of candy were so tempting, I wanted to grab a handful to take to my room. Instead, I said, slow and distinct, so I wouldn't be misunderstood, "Mr. Porter, I promise I will not play cards with Toby or Eliot again. Is that what you wanted me to say?"

Mr. Porter leaned against the fridge and shook his head. Kept shaking his head.

After a couple more shakes, I realized he was off thinking about something else. Or remembering something from his childhood. Probably playing the gambling discussion over in his head and trying to figure out how to say everything a different way. Or how he would tell it to his sister or to his golf buddies.

I turned on the ball of my foot and marched upstairs.

ELIOT

Halloween night, and Marj was late getting home. Road construction again, she said.

She charged through the house, yelling up to me that we would leave in five minutes.

I was ready. And waiting. I rushed downstairs.

A few seconds later, Marj came out of her room. From her hand dangled three black facemasks. The kind that only covers your eyes and nose. "I didn't know," she said, "what kind of costume you wanted. At lunch, I went to a costume store, but it was so crowded. So, I just–"

She stopped. She had pulled on a yellowish-brown T-shirt that had mussed her hair, and she looked even more like a lonely scarecrow.

Marj had actually thought about me during the day. And she had tried. Surprised, I found a smile on my face.

It was enough. She had tried.

I took two masks from her hand, one for me and one for Alli. "You have to wear your mask while we're at the Community Center. The whole time you're in the Bread Project booth. Okay?"

"I'll do it." She slipped on the mask and her eyes twinkled from inside the dark cutouts. "And after, I'll drive you and your friends around to do some trick-or-treating. Okay?"

I took a deep breath, suddenly full of hope. "Thanks."

"Well. Good." Now, Marj was embarrassed and couldn't look at me. "Okay. Let's get going. Gotta pick up Alli." She almost ran through the kitchen, stopping only to grab a small bag of pretzels, and hustled out to the car.

At Mr. Porter's house, Marj pulled in the driveway and stopped. "Hurry," she said.

I jumped out of the car and galumphed up to the door, too happy to merely jog or trot. This was going to be a good night.

Two jack-o-lanterns sat on the front step, casting a flickering light. Creepy sounds–squeaks, screams, and moans–blared from small speakers. Pretty lame, but–hey, Mr. Porter was trying. And tonight, trying counted.

A tall, cloaked figure opened the door. From deep within the hood, Mr. Porter's voice croaked, "Welcome to our haunted castle."

I grinned and played along. "Trick-or-treat!"

Mr. Porter shoved back the hood and looked me up and down. "Where's the costume?"

For a second, when Mr. Porter's pockmarked face appeared, I thought of werewolves and Beauty and the Beast and other stories that explained ugly faces. I didn't know if I should shudder or laugh. So, I just went ahead, still playing along.

"It's a joke." I made Vs with my fingers, and put one finger on my eyebrow, the other under my eye, on either side, in a fake mask. "I'm disguised. As a sixth grader."

Mr. Porter raised an eyebrow, and this time, I did want to laugh. I could've played along a bit more, but Marj was in a hurry.

Dropping my hands and smiling, I asked, "Is Alli ready?"

"For what?"

"We're going to the Harvest Party at the Community Center."

"She didn't ask permission for that."

"But–" I stopped, suddenly remembering who I was talking to. Mr. Porter, the sixth grade social studies teacher who never smiled except on Halloween night when he played up the scary stuff.

I stepped back and waved for Marj to come to the door.

She slipped the car into park and turned off the engine. Half-pulled herself out of the car. Called, "What's wrong?"

I only waved at her to come.

Mr. Porter stepped outside, too, and closed the door. "Don't want the house to get cold."

When Marj stopped at the bottom of the steps, Mr. Porter said, "Now, what's going on tonight?"

"The Community Center Harvest Party. We have a booth for the Bread Project, and Alli is supposed to come and help."

"Oh. That project." Mr. Porter knelt and took the top off a jack-o-lantern, letting the candle throw deep, sharp shadows over his creepy face. "It's a waste of time."

All my elation fell away.

Apparently, satisfied that the candle would burn a while longer, he replaced the jack-o-lantern's top. He straightened up and stared at Marj. "It won't work. People won't bake bread and won't bring it for Thanksgiving."

Now, his gray face almost disappeared against the gray concrete of the house. Like a ghost fading in and out, that's what he looked like. I shivered.

"Thanks for the warning," Marj said. Her voice wasn't melting chocolate anymore: it was as sharp as an icicle. "But we're doing the Bread Project anyway. And Alli has volunteered to help. Volunteered. If you don't mind."

From a block or so away, we heard kids yelling. Mr. Porter pulled his hood back up and muttered, "A bread project."

At his sarcasm, Marj took a step up. She held her body tense, like a rubber band stretched to its limits. "You don't mind if Alli helps, do you? Because the Project is to honor the memory of my husband."

A lump filled my throat: sadness that Griff was gone, yet pride that Marj was standing up there, defiant, fighting for Griff's memory. I stepped up beside her.

Mr. Porter returned her stare. Then abruptly, he dropped his eyes.

The laughter from the trick-or-treaters echoed through the neighborhood. They were just two houses away.

Mr. Porter jerked open the door and called. "Come on down. You're trying to listen anyway."

Alli clattered down the wooden stairs and out the door to stand beside Marj.

"You'll bring her home later? I won't have to get out and pick her up?"

"I'll bring her home," Marj said.

Walking out to the car, I said, "Guess what Marj brought us?" I pulled out the masks.

"Oh. I bought masks, too." She held up her two masks.

Suddenly, we were laughing and piling into the car. Happy.

Behind us, the group of kids had reached Mr. Porter's house, and we heard his voice croak, "Welcome to our haunted castle!"

"Trick-or-treat!"

❖

Walking into the community center, it was already crowded. The Halloween booths were already decorated and people were chattering, gossiping, smiling. I saw Toby at his Dad's political booth and waved.

We had to ask several people before we found someone in charge, who sent us to find the janitor, who led us to the back of the gymnasium. He pushed up his wire-rims, turned away slightly and sneezed. "Sorry, I must be getting a cold." He rubbed his nose again, trying to keep back another sneeze.

I put my hands behind my back and stepped away.

Meanwhile, the janitor stopped at a booth and gestured. I stared at the blue curtains that created a small booth space. The other booths were lined up in the aisles, like the setup for the back-to-school party. But the Bread Project booth was on a far wall. Far away from everything else. Separated by a huge empty floor space, an ocean to cross to get to our booth.

"This is our booth?" Marj demanded.

"Your sign up said this was a Bread Project." The janitor pushed up his wire-rims again. "Most food booths want to be close to the kitchen."

Marj and Mrs. Lopez looked at each other and then back at the janitor.

"There's nothing else?" Marj asked.

"Not tonight." The janitor turned and walked away.

Mrs. Patel looked back at the aisles of booths, then at ours. "We don't have anything to decorate with, either." Today, she'd come straight from work: black skirt, white shirt and heels.

I sat cross-legged on the floor. "No one will find us over here." This was a big setback for the project. I was afraid to look at Marj, to see her disappointment.

By now, we realized that we had to contact the parents; without them, the project was dead. Kids just didn't understand it exactly, how important it was to pass off the sourdough starter on time each week. They didn't understand enough about baking. And then, there was the question of who would buy the bread. The auction needed community people who would buy bread as a donation to the school.

The aisles were full of costumed figures: a David and Goliath walking along together, several wore the latest store-bought Batman costume, and some poor kid who had decided to actually wear a World War I wool uniform. I felt sorry for him.

Mrs. Johnson set down her basket of supplies and bread and put her hands on her hips. "Maybe, maybe not. We've made a mistake, not getting a better booth, not setting up early. But we're just learning. It happens."

"*Si*. Let's get set up, and while we work, we can decide what to do," Mrs. Lopez said.

Alli stepped up then. "Good. And while you work, you have to wear a mask." She passed out the masks, and everyone put them on. Somehow it was easier to smile with a mask on your face.

I finally looked at Marj, and she even tried a smile. She nodded at me to help her with our boxes that held a couple loaves of bread. I heaved them onto the table top and lined up the loaves. Soon, the table was heaping with breads.

Mrs. Lopez had *pan dulce*, a Mexican sweet bread; Mrs. Patel had her *naan*; and Mrs. Johnson had made cinnamon rolls. Lots of great samples, lots of brochures to pass out, just no one to give them out to. I pulled the mask back over my face and wished the evening was over.

ALLI

Trouble, that's what we had. The mothers were cute in their masks, hurrying around getting brochures and bread laid out and in order. But after that, they were clueless, totally without ideas.

I squinted, looking from our booth to the aisles of games. How could you get someone to come over here, just to pick up a brochure?

You couldn't. Tonight, everyone was thinking about costumes and candy and fun.

I saw a few tutus and capes pass by. Nothing special. Then, Sam came out of one aisle, heading for the next. Dressed in a turban and wide flowing pants. Ali Baba, I guess. He waved, but moved on to a basketball toss. A second later, Toby waved, too, dressed as Michael Jackson. Really strange for a blond kid to dress like the King of Pop, but somehow, Toby's walk carried it off.

I fiddled with my mask. The elastic rubber band had caught and tangled my hair. Mrs. Patel noticed what I was doing and took a step over to help me straighten it. And I said, "Thanks for your help."

"No problem," she said. "Any time."

And that made me think about all the times I'd heard someone say something like that. I know. Mostly people just say that to be polite or because they are paid to say it. Like Mrs. Brodie-Rock saying to call her anytime.

But the Bread Project was different. Mrs. Patel really was working on the cookbook and Mrs. Johnson had joined us and had already visited a couple families, talking recipes and such. Mrs. Zane had done the brochures to pass out to parents. Seems like the project was something that people wanted to help with. Really help. Like I really wanted it to succeed.

I clenched my fists. Well, now was the time. We needed help. People wouldn't come to our booth, but –

I turned toward the booth and said loudly, "I know what to do."

All eyes turned to me.

"What?" Eliot sounded harsh. Despite his mask and the party, he was frowning.

"We take the bread to them." I explained that we'd gather up some other sixth graders, and then we'd walk up and down the aisles and give away small bread samples and the brochures.

Mrs. Winston ran a hand through her bangs. It was still rare to hear her laugh, but she wasn't quite as sad anymore. I think the project had helped. When she wasn't around, Mrs. Lopez said the project had helped Mrs. Winston a lot, making her meet people and work with them and not stay at home all the time.

"Well, it might work," Mrs. Winston said.

"I brought a knife," Mrs. Johnson said. "I can cut each cinnamon rolls into three or four pieces."

The others nodded, and it was agreed.

I waved at Eliot to come with me. "Let's find some help while they get the samples ready."

Walking beside me, Eliot scowled. "This is stupid."

I didn't really think it would work, either. After all, it was Halloween. But we were desperate to get people to pay attention to the Bread Project and had to try something. Or else pack it up and go home. My fist clenched again at that thought. We couldn't give up. Not when I was starting to see how the community could come together on this.

When we found Toby and Sam and explained it, they were excited.

"Giving away something is always fun," Toby said.

We asked them to find a couple other kids who might help and meet us at the Bread Project booth.

Ten minutes later, Toby, Sam, Marisa, Brad and a couple others–about a dozen altogether–scattered into the crowd, carrying brochures and bread samples to pass out.

We had just done one simple thing. Ask for help. Is that all it took, you just had to ask? I was stunned.

ELIOT

The lanes of booths were packed now, and the large room was filled with a low roar. I fixed my mask in place, grabbed the napkins Alli held out, and started to follow her.

But she had other ideas: "Everyone split up and try to give away everything in your basket. Meet back here in ten minutes. We'll see how we're doing."

I nodded and turned toward the left aisle.

"Bread! Free bread samples!" Alli called.

Heading for the middle aisle, Toby started bellowing, "Free! Get your sample bread here! Free!"

So, I did the same: "Free bread!"

A short, bald man stopped and stared, trying to see behind my mask. "Eliot Winston?"

I lifted my mask and nodded.

"I thought so." The man pulled me into a tight hug.

Whoa, what an aftershave smell. Spicy and strong. I squirmed and tried to breathe.

The man suddenly sneezed, trying, but failing to cover his mouth.

I cringed and stepped back.

From behind his fat hand, the man mumbled, "Griff was a great man. Sure miss him."

I watched the man's germ-laden hand, making sure it didn't come near me. "Um, how did you know Griff?"

"Just around the community. You tell Mrs. Winston, tell her that we miss him."

The man reached out to pat my shoulder, but I ducked down and put a brochure in his hand instead.

"Sure, I'll tell her." I scooted away. After a dozen steps, I looked back. He was still reading the brochure.

"Free bread!" I called.

Another man stopped. He was skinny and unshaven. Thin cheeks, thin hands. I had to squirm away from another hug and decided that aftershave lotion was better than the unwashed smell.

And a woman had to hug me—sweet, flowery perfume—and say how sorry she was for our loss.

I finally realized that I hadn't been to the Community Center since Griff had died three months ago. School and work, that's all Marj and I did. How many people did Griff know, anyway?

I asked the next hugger that question.

The large—and we're talking really large—red-headed woman widened her eyes, "Why, Griff helped just about every person here, at one time or another. Most times you didn't need to even ask for help. Griff just knew."

I thought about that. Griff had always been busy doing this or that for someone, it was true. But he'd never seemed to be flustered or overworked or anything like that. It was just as natural as breathing in and out for him. "Thanks. I just didn't know so many people loved him."

"Too bad you didn't know," she said. "'Cause he was special."

"We're doing a project at school in Griff's honor." I handed her a brochure.

She glanced at it, then stuck it in a bag hanging from her arm. "We do the Halloween Carnival, but otherwise, well, we don't get involved with the school much."

"That's okay," I said politely and tried to move on. But I had to dodge another hug.

Finally, she moved on. But behind me a big sneeze erupted, followed by a chorus of "Bless you." Spinning around, I saw the redhead woman rub her freckled nose with the back of her fat hand. She saw me and smiled and waved again.

I shivered. It was cold season, all right.

By now, over ten minutes had passed, so I headed back. I wove through the crowd. Crossed the ocean of empty space. Dragged myself up on the deserted island of the Bread Project booth.

Even with the extra kids helping, it looked like we had already surrendered. The women were just sitting on metal chairs, not even talking; just staring across the empty space at the busy booths. Marj still had on her black mask. It didn't hide her sadness, but it did prevent her from making eye contact with the others.

They all reminded me of third grade, the year I tried soccer, and the team was the worst ever, losing every game except one. One game we lost by a score of 15-0. It was a complete team failure. Never played again. This Bread Project team didn't have much of a chance, either. The Project was going to fail.

Nor did Alli or Toby or Sam or Marisa or anyone have much encouragement.

"Kids are eating candy. Not bread."

"No one wants our flyers. If they take a flyer, I find it on the floor later."

"What can we do?" I asked.

"We'll try again," Alli said. She took up her basket and flyers again and tiptoed across the open space like she was walking on water. As she disappeared into the crowd, we heard her call, "Free bread!"

Toby sighed and said, "Well, working together, we can finish fast and then go trick-or-treating. I bet three chocolate bars that I can hand out more than you."

It was the only thing that sent me back into the aisles. I loved chocolate, and I could never turn down a bet from Toby.

We spent the next thirty minutes hawking bread samples. Picking up flyers people had dropped and putting them in someone else's hand. No real progress, but we tried.

By the end of it all, we were tired, and ready to get out of the Community Center. We cleaned and packed up quickly, then divided up into three cars to finally go trick-or-treating.

ALLI

Sitting between Mrs. Winston and Eliot, I had to hold myself very still. Inside, I was trembling with excitement. Trick-or-treating. Every kid in America has done it; every kid but me.

It wasn't a specific candy I wanted. It wasn't the costume that excited me. It was the experience, the living through an event that every other kid took for granted. It was this longing for normal that I could never quite fulfill. All I knew was this: normal kids trick-or-treated and laughed and traded candy. Talked about the awful toothbrushes they got at one house, and the load of chocolate at another.

Mrs. Winston stopped at one street, and the other two cars pulled up behind us, Mrs. Lopez in her van, and Mrs. Johnson in her truck. We all piled out together, pushing and shoving, waiting for someone to start toward a house.

Finally, I pointed to the brick one before us. "Let's go."

We charged, laughing and calling, but I got there first. Rang the doorbell. Was the first to yell, "Trick-or-treat." The first to hold out my bag, the first to get some candy. Now this–this was fun.

Later, after an hour of trick-or-treating, Mrs. Winston dropped off everyone else at their homes and turned toward the Porter's house.

"Would you just look?" I scooped up handfuls of candy and let them fall back into my bag. What a night.

Eliot held up a caramel. "Want to trade for some chocolate?"

Sure. I got every caramel and sour thing he had, plus all the candy corn. In return, I gave him all my chocolate. Didn't like it anyway, so it worked out.

Finally, we stopped at the Porter's house. I stepped out, then turned back. "Mrs. Winston? Do you know how kind you are? This is the best Halloween I've ever had. Thanks."

Her brow furrowed, like she was puzzled. "A simple mask and some candy? Is that all it takes to make this a special Halloween?"

Eliot looked up at the ceiling, and I saw him swallow. And I understood.

I reached in and pulled out the largest bag of candy corn I had gotten. Solemn now, I held it out to her. When she shook her head, I put it on the seat beside her anyway.

"Really. Tonight–" I blinked back tears. "–this was special. Thanks."

Then, because I couldn't hold it back any longer, I turned and ran into Mr. Porter's house, up the stairs to Tim's room and threw myself on the itchy blanket and burst into tears of happiness.

BREAD PROJECT: WEEK 7

ELIOT

Signs. What does one innocent sign tell about a person, about a family? For example a "For Sale" sign, like the one in front of the white house where I live, the house that had belonged to Griff and before him, to Griff's aunt. What would a "For Sale" sign there mean? What did it say about the family in the house?

It said Change was coming.

But a sign couldn't say if that Change would be good or bad. Or, maybe Change could be both good and bad. Change might be good for the kids, but bad for the adults.

Or vice versa.

Here's the math: 1 For Sale sign + 2 persons trying to make a family = Change.

I didn't know how to stop the math of Change. Change was coming. Ready or not.

That Saturday morning, it started with a phone call from Miss Clay saying that she wanted to show the house twice that afternoon: that is, if Marj and I could be out of the house from 1-3 pm, then she could show it at that time.

I put down my orange juice glass, letting the morning sun try to reach through the juice to the table. I shoved back my half-full bowl of cereal. "Today? We're not finished with painting."

In truth, the breakfast room was still yellow, but everything else was white. My room had smelled of oil paint last night, so I'd left the windows open a crack, and by now, the house was finally starting to smell just fresh and new instead of like oil paint.

"Yes we are. I'll light some scented candles for a couple hours, and that will help the smell. We are ready to show the house." Marj scooped up the breakfast dishes and carried them to the kitchen. I followed.

"Who is looking at our house today?"

"The first person is the gentleman who wanted to know the size of the attic. The second is a young couple getting married at

Christmas who want a home to come back to after their honeymoon."

I dumped my cereal and juice into the disposal. Flipped the switch and let the loud disposal bury Marj's chatter. Slammed my dishes into the dishwasher. Wishing, wishing, wishing I could stop this. "Where will we go for two hours?'

Marj leaned over the counter and something—a stillness in her—made me look up.

"I want," she said, "to visit Griff's grave. The stone is in, and I want to be sure it was done right. I was going to just go out there alone. But—maybe—well, maybe you want to come, too?"

A gravestone and a For Sale sign. Both signs of Change.

That July week—the one when Griff died—had been bookended with birds.

On Monday, Griff and Marj and I ate an early breakfast. Carried our plates to the glass table on the deck, enjoying the relatively cool morning air that would soon heat to a humid summer afternoon in the mid-south. Below the deck, poking around in the grass, were mourning doves. Coo-coo-cooing. Crooning to each other of the eggs in the nest. Singing of the family that would soon hatch. Or so it seemed to me.

Everything that morning was tinged with family and love and joy.

By 9 am, Griff and I were dressed. Sports coats—mine was new from the wedding—dress shirts and ties. Marj wore a dress and heels, her long hair in a ponytail. Sunday best clothes for this special day.

Griff pulled the Toyota Camry out of the garage, and I opened the door for Marj with a bow. She flashed me a smile and waved a manila envelope. "It's a big day for me, too," she said.

At the courthouse, we took things slowly. Stopped to smell long-stemmed yellow roses in the rose garden. Stopped to tilt back our heads to study the golden honeycomb pattern of the stained glass dome. Stopped outside the courtroom and asked a bystander to take our picture under the Judge's name. Sat quietly, waiting for the judge to call our case. Held hands as the judge signed the adoption order, making our family official, making Griff my Dad, and making me his son. Smiled at anyone and everyone. Stopped to file the adoption papers for Marj to become my Mom.

Outside, on the other side of the courthouse, hummingbirds darted to feeders, sipped and flitted to the next feeder. I watched, transfixed by the bird's green and ruby red iridescent feathers and graceful flying. I felt like my heart was fluttering about, too. Like it might burst with joy at any moment. We celebrated with triple scoop cones at the ice cream store across the street, then went back to the car.

Griff stopped beside the driver's side and closed his left eye. "Marj, maybe you should drive. The cold of that ice cream has given me a headache."

Marj took the keys, while Griff went around the car. He stumbled, but caught himself and said, "Just the curb," and climbed in.

I frowned, but Griff seemed okay, and he did have headaches a lot.

I slouched back, still in a happy daze, thinking of how I would sign my name at school the next year, Eliot Winston. At home, I'd find some paper and practice.

Traffic was light, a weekday and just mid-morning. I watched the skyscrapers and bridges pass-by and was startled when Marj said sharply, "Griff!"

I leaned forward. Griff's head had slumped; his chin rested on his chest.

"What's wrong?" I asked.

Marj was breathing fast. "He just passed out."

"What's wrong?" I asked again, "What's wrong?"

That day, that beautiful, happy day. It took on a brilliant look, as if a crystal-clear magnifying glass had suddenly appeared. Griff's face was pale. A drop of chocolate ice cream stained the white collar of his dress shirt. The diamond of Marj's wedding ring flashed in the sunshine. Then the day turned dark. Like someone had closed a curtain on an act in a play.

Marj gripped the steering wheel tightly. "Something's not right. We're going to the ER."

For some reason, I always remembered that. She said, "ER" and not "Emergency Room."

Lights and bustle, nurses and antiseptic smells—the ER and the whole hospital confused me. For three long, weary days and nights, we waited, Marj and I. Waited for Griff to wake up. But the brain tumor took him late on Wednesday night.

And on Friday, we were at the cemetery. Someone lowered a black casket into a dirt hole. Unable to watch any longer, I focused on a tall, almost leafless tree that hovered over the small chapel, a chapel with a dome of golden honeycomb stained glass. That morning, we had prayed in that chapel for Griff's soul.

I stared at the tree that hovered over the dome. A movement caught my attention, the head of a small cat. I blinked. Cats didn't climb that far up a tree.

Then the minister finished praying, and the crowd—so many people that they filled the entire cemetery–everyone started singing a hymn. So many people, all singing a hymn for Griff and he couldn't even hear it.

I blinked again. Marj had had a husband for three weeks. I had only had a father for three days.

The cat in the treetop rose, like it was climbing even higher. Tufts, feather tufts came out of its ears. The cat spread wide wings, almost as wide as I could reach. Eyes riveted now, I realized it was a Great Horned owl. The crowd started singing a final hymn, "Amazing Grace." And the owl launched into the air and flew straight at me, swerving at the last second to swoop straight over Griff's grave, hooting softly, "Hoo-hoo hooooo hoo-hoo," saying good-night and good-bye to the kindest man who had ever lived, an honorary fly-over acknowledging that with the passing of Griffith Winston, the universe had changed forever.

Now, the first day of November—All Saints Day, Alli had told me it was called—the cemetery looked about the same as in July, except the leaves were in full autumn colors. Orange, yellow, and rusty brown leaves carpeted most of the graves, marking the passing of yet another season. Three full months without Griff, it seemed impossible that time passed so fast.

Marj, in jeans and a long-sleeved T-shirt, knelt beside the stone and read.

"Griffith Winston
Beloved Father and Husband"

"It looks good, doesn't it?" she asked.

I shrugged. "Sure." It was gray granite, just like every other stone in the cemetery. Why did everyone choose gray? Griff wouldn't have liked the sad color.

"I'm going to change the flowers," Marj said. From the vase near the stone, she pulled out the brown – the dead – flowers. "Throw these in that trash can." She handed them to me and motioned toward a trashcan near the chapel. Then she unwrapped the mums and daisies she had brought.

I took the brown flowers in my fingertips and held them far away from my body. Didn't seem right. Dead flowers in this place where dead people slept. We should have brought fake flowers.

I walked toward the chapel and the owl's tree. I threw away the flowers, then kicked the leaves under the tree. I couldn't see the owl's nest; it was too high up. But I found pellets, crumbled and dry. I kicked one and tiny bones flew apart. Probably rodents the owl had eaten. We were studying biology in science class. Maybe I should take one back to Miss Garrett. Just the sort of thing she'd like.

Across the cemetery, Marj's cell phone rang. I stood and watched her talking. Was it Miss Clay? Did someone want to buy our house? Marj nodded a few times, then put up her phone and knelt to finish arranging the flowers.

I wanted to race to Marj and ask what Miss Clay had said. But I decided that bad news could keep. Instead, I went to the car and found a plastic bag from some store and gathered pellets. I stopped now and then to crane my neck upward, looking for the owl. But I didn't see it.

When I had eight or ten good pellets, I looked for Marj. She was leaning backwards on the hood of the car, just watching me.

I walked over and said, "I found owl pellets. Miss Garrett, the science teacher, will like them."

Marj flushed. "Oh. I almost forgot the owl, how it flew over that day." She held the bag up to eye height and shook it gently. "This is owl poop? And Miss Garrett is your science teacher?"

I nodded yes to both questions. Marj hadn't paid much attention this year to my teachers' names.

"Well. It's Miss Garrett that we need to talk about," she said.

Confused, I said, "What?"

"She's engaged."

"Everyone knows that." From the first day of school, that's all she had talked about. I hadn't minded because many days it meant no homework.

"Well," Marj said, "she's engaged and that means she's getting married."

"Yes." I still wasn't getting it.

"And she and Shane Baxter, her fiancé, have made an offer on the house."

I froze. Couldn't say anything. Couldn't frown. Couldn't smile. Couldn't even blink.

Marj took the plastic bag from my hand and set it on the car's hood. "Don't get excited about it, yet. The first buyer decided on a different house, so he's out of it. And Miss Garrett and Mr. Baxter made a contingent offer. That means he's got to sell his house first, and then we can decide if we want to sign the papers to sell our house. Nothing is decided yet because it might take months for Baxter's house to sell. Meanwhile, we can still take offers from others."

She told me not to get excited, but her voice was excited. She was glad we had this offer on our house. Sell the house. Send the kid off to foster care. And she'd have her life back again.

Suddenly, I sneezed. Which made my eyes water. I sneezed again, bending almost double, turning away and mumbling, "Excuse me."

My head hurt, too. I rubbed my forehead, then my temples, and stared at the fall leaves covering the graves. Dead leaves covering dead hopes.

"Are you okay?' Marj asked.

I straightened, stiffened my back and turned. "Fine. I'm ready to go—" I couldn't finish the sentence, couldn't say go home, could I? " – ready to go back to the house."

"You don't look good. Maybe you're allergic to something out here. You didn't see any poison ivy did you?" She handed me the bag of owl pellets, then got into the car and drove.

But the house, the possibility that it might sell, had her too excited. She kept coming back to details that needed to be finished before it sold. "But surely it will sell," she said, "even if the trim work in the sun room still needs a second coat."

I let her talk, leaning my hot forehead against the cool window.

She was saying: "Miss Clay will come by later with some papers for me to sign. She said Miss Garrett loved the fresh white paint, and Mr. Baxter loved the upstairs room because he's a part-time taxidermist. He stays busy mounting deer heads and things like that, and he'll set them up in that room. It's perfect for them. I'm so glad we got everything in such good order because they are offering full price."

I couldn't believe it. My room, my bedroom. Turned into a workroom for a taxidermist, a room with lots of stuffed dead things. Somehow, it seemed inevitable.

ALLI

How many ways can you spell S-T-U-P-I-D? And still get it wrong?

Why, why, why, why, why had I asked for an allowance? All it did was get Mr. Porter riled up. He was supposed to do grocery shopping this morning because we were out of cereal and orange juice and bread. But he was already out on a golf date when I came downstairs. I licked my peanut butter jar clean and then there was nothing.

Hunger gnawed at my stomach and I'd get nothing at home. Miss Porter was out working, as usual. And as soon as Mr. Porter left for golf, I left, too. Eliot had better come through for me.

But no one was home. No one.

Pumpkins and pots of fall flowers—yellow, bronze and burgundy – sat on the front porch. Why had Mrs. Winston dolled up the place? She had done nothing earlier that fall and nothing for Halloween. Why now?

I sat on the front porch and leaned, wrapping one arm around the column and one around my tight stomach. And waited.

Finally, thirty minutes later, Mrs. Winston and Eliot arrived home. I walked around to the garage to talk to Eliot. His jaw was tight, his brows furrowed—Eliot was mad about something. He glanced at me and stormed toward the back yard.

I didn't care. I grabbed his arm and made him stop.

"What?" Now he was mad at me.

Looking back to Mrs. Winston, who was watching us, I whispered. "What's wrong with you?"

"What do you want?"

My stomach answered with a loud rumble.

Eliot did a tight shake of his head. "Not now."

"Eliot, I'm hungry."

He looked away, toward the back yard.

"Mr. Porter left me with nothing to eat. I've had nothing at all today." Well, he didn't have to know about the spoonful of peanut butter; that was barely anything. "You promised."

Eliot's shoulders sagged, and he said. "Okay. Come on in."

ELIOT

By now, I'm an expert in boxed mac and cheese meals. I could cook one in my sleep. I can even cook one when I'm so sad and mad that I want to just curl up and bury my head under the covers. Because no matter how I felt, I couldn't leave Alli to starve to death.

Marj must have known I was upset, but with Alli there, she ignored it. While I cooked the mac and cheese, Marj set the table. I searched the cupboards for something to add to the meal and ended up with animal crackers, and, of course pretzels. Water to drink.

While Alli bit the heads off various animals, Marj chattered and crunched on pretzels. Alli started lining up her headless animals, and Marj tried to bite off just part of the pretzel to form the ABCs. In the midst of all this, Marj talked. Told all about Miss Clay, Miss Garrett and Shane Baxter. The offer on the house.

Allie's eyes got bigger and bigger. She glanced my way, bit off an elephant's head, laid down the elephant body, glanced at me again.

Somehow, my stomach didn't hurt as much, just knowing she understood.

Meanwhile, I opened a can of peaches, pulled out some miniature carrots and ranch dressing.

Finally, I served the mac and cheese. Thing is, in the whole kitchen, nothing smelled like food. We had a full meal that didn't smell at all.

Marj ate half the peaches, a small spoonful of mac and cheese and one carrot. Then she went to her office, carrying the pretzel bag with her.

As soon as she was out of sight, Alli leaned forward. She spoke low, making sure her voice didn't carry to Marj's study. "You're mad about the offer on the house."

"Duh."

"Did you tell her you don't want her to sell it?"

"She knows that."

At Alli's silence, I repeated, "She knows. She has to know."

"Did you tell her?"

"No."

"So, you're just giving up?"

I closed my eyes, ignoring Alli. I was just sitting there, trying hard not to think of anything, but of course, that meant I was thinking of everything. Like Marj about to sell the house. About the Bread Project doing so badly at the Halloween party.

Suddenly, I heard a thump and opened my eyes.

Alli had hopped down from the stool, and now, she grabbed the back of my chair and tipped me out!

I sprawled on the floor and stared at her, outraged. "Why—"

But she cut me off, standing over me and glaring. "Get up! Let's go to your room." She whirled, marched across the living room and stomped up the stairs.

While I scrambled to my feet, I called after her, "What's wrong with you?"

Marj suddenly appeared in the doorway of her office. "Everything okay?"

I froze.

Then, my jaw tightened. She knew what was wrong. I wasn't going to say it. "Yes, ma'am. We're okay."

"Is Alli okay?"

"Yes, we were just playing around."

"Well, don't get too rough." And she went back to her office.

I took the stairs two at a time. Alli was sitting cross-legged in a patch of sunshine.

I sank beside her. "What's wrong with you?" But this time, I spoke softly, drained of energy.

"You, that's what's wrong. You had a great dad and now you have a mom, and she's great, too. And you're letting her get rid of you without even fighting."

I groaned. Didn't want to listen to her harsh washing-machine voice. It sounded the worst when she was mad like this. "If Marj doesn't want me, what can I do?"

"She's sad, too. She's scared. You could let her know how important this is to you. You have a chance. For a real family." Her voice choked, and she suddenly stood and went to lean on the windowsill to look out at the street. Now her voice turned really harsh. "I'm a foster kid. But you're practically a Son."

I heard the capital letter she gave to Son.

With hand on hips, she turned and glared. "You have to fight for your family."

And I fought back. "Yeah. Like you fought for yours. Did you ever try to find your dad yourself?"

Alli's mouth hung open. "What?"

"Did. You. Ever. Try. To. Find. Your. Dad?" I took a certain satisfaction in her shock at the question.

"They tried to find him. He's dead. Just like your dad."

I winced at that one. But I'd been thinking about this too long to shut up now. "Maybe, maybe not. I looked on the Internet. They publish names of soldiers killed in action."

"What?"

"His name isn't there. If I were you, I'd fight for my family, too. I'd look all over the Internet and try to find my dad. Lots of places to find people. Especially old Army guys."

Alli waved her hand, chasing dust caught in the sunbeams. "Look for him myself?"

"Yes."

"I never even thought of it."

"I can help you do that," I said. Didn't tell her that I'd already been poking around for more than soldiers killed in action, finding places with information on living ones. "I've learned a lot, working on the website about Griff."

Alli shook her head. "You want me to find my dad, but you won't work hard to save your family?"

We stood there, staring at each other. Staring at golden dust floating down. Staring at dreams that wouldn't die.

Finally, I said, "I don't know what to say to Marj. But I can help you look for your dad."

"And I don't know how to look for my dad. But I can help you with Marj. Maybe we can help each other? Do you want to try?"

I looked around my room. I wanted this bedroom to be mine forever. I didn't want it filled with deer heads or fish mounted on boards. Dead things. "Yes," I whispered. "I want to try."

❖

Alli and I talked for a while but didn't make any solid plans. When she left, I lay on my bed and thought. Dreamed. Hoped. Despaired.

Then, practical—as every kid who's ever been a foster child must be practical—I got up and searched in my closet to find my duffle bag. I found a small box and filled it with pictures of Griff. Monday, after school when Marj was gone, I'd go around and get pictures of Griff and use Marj's scanner to make copies of everything. Then I'd burn a disk of pictures and put it in my duffle bag. Or maybe, I'd put them on the memorial website I was doing for Griff, where no one could take them away from me. Yeah, that would be better.

Either way, I'd start packing this bag with important things. Ready for the day after Thanksgiving. Just in case.

And I'd try to save $100 by then, too. Didn't want to be like Alli, a foster kid with no money. Yeah. I'd let Alli try to help me with Marj. But just in case, I'd be ready to take care of myself.

"Is it true?" Toby leaned his elbow on the table and rested his head on his hand, like he was tired. "You gave Miss Garrett some poop?"

The noise swirled around us, with kids coming and going, chatting and calling. It was the usual garbage-in, garbage-out school cafeteria with concrete block walls and easy to mop floors.

"Yep." I grinned, and put my tray beside Toby's and pulled a chair beside him. I had enjoyed the poop joke all morning.

"You gave her POOP? Are you crazy?"

"It was owl pellets. Technically, poop. They're all furry, like the owl ate one mouse per pellet." It was Thursday, our day for science labs, so I had waited till today to take in the owl pellets. Miss Garrett had planned some smelly chemistry project, but she was glad to put it off until next week and do the pellets today. "I expect we'll find at least one entire mouse skeleton. Owls can swallow a mouse whole." Would he understand that I wanted to bet?

Toby took a deep breath and closed his eyes.

"What's wrong?" I asked.

"Don't feel good."

His tanned face was paler than usual. And he looked sweaty. But nothing else.

"Are you going to eat that burger?" Alli sat down opposite Toby.

Without looking, Toby pushed his orange tray toward her. "Go ahead."

Alli took a huge bite, and with her mouth full, asked me, "You gave Miss Garrett some poop?"

This joke was just too good.

Toby said, "Owl pellets. He wants to bet we'll find at least one entire mouse skeleton." He shook his head. "But I'm tired of bets."

She said, "You beat me all the time. Besides, it's just friendly bets."

I exchanged looks with Alli. She wasn't playing cards any more, but sometimes she took on other bets. Quietly.

"Well, I don't bet on poop." Toby yawned.

"You'll be betting on mouse skeletons," I said, "not poop." In the next few weeks, I needed to save $100 so I'd have money at the new foster family. It wasn't a good time for Toby to get tired of betting. "But we don't have to bet. If you want to stop gambling your hard-earned allowance, it's nothing to me."

"Yeah." Alli raised her eyebrows at me, as if to question the wisdom of this statement. "We don't want to bet."

Toby shoved his chair out a foot, leaned back, stuck his hands in his jeans pockets and let his legs stretch out under the table. "Well, I like to bet, you know that. I don't mind losing either. But sometimes, I just want to win. Just now and then. Just one bet."

"Okay," I said. "Suggest something."

"I bet I get sick before the end of the day."

"Aw, that's not a fair bet. You'll make yourself puke." There had been lots of kids out this week with some sort of stomach virus. But not many in sixth grade, mostly little kids.

"No, really," he said. "And it's one bet I hope I don't win."

An itch ran down my spine. I scooted my chair to the end of the table, away from Toby. Under the table, I found my napkin. Wiped my hands off.

"That's right," Toby said. "Keep away from me, or you'll catch it."

I shuddered. I might catch it.

But Alli said, "If you're sick and not eating. . ."

Toby just shrugged and waved his entire tray toward Alli. He leaned back, closed his eyes, and within a couple minutes, he was asleep. Right there. In the middle of the cafeteria noise. Sleeping.

Alli and I ate without talking. Just watching Toby and worrying.

Ring! Ring! Ring!

The bell was loud, but Toby didn't move.

I stood, and Alli motioned at Toby. I shook my head. No way was I going to touch him.

She walked around the table and shook his shoulder. "Bell. Time for science."

Toby drew in a ragged breath and yawned. "Thanks. I'll be there."

I backed off to let him pass me and watched him go to the boy's bathroom. This was one bet I didn't want to win, either.

I strolled to class, not wanting to get there early. Miss Garrett had talked to me every day about our house. I didn't want to hear how Shane Baxter loved Griff's garage, or how much Miss Garrett loved Griff's kitchen.

Timed it perfect. Slipped into the chair behind Alli just as the bell rang.

At the lab tables in the back, Miss Garrett had the owl pellets set up. She divided the class into eight groups, each with its own fuzzy pellet.

My group—with three girls—insisted I dissect. I snapped on the plastic gloves. Then, I tried to pick up and use the needle-sharp tool and tweezers. I was clumsy. The girls giggled, but I ignored them. Finally, Marissa Blue, who had just become the starting catcher for the girls' softball team, reached over and put the tools in my hands.

I nodded at her, and then bent over the pellet. Eased it apart, working slow and careful, pulling out tiny, pale bones.

Marissa got interested and found another pair of tweezers and tried to line up the bones in a skeleton shape. This was fun. Rib bone, leg bone, back bone—it might really be a full skeleton. But where was the skull?

Then, Toby called out, his voice all weird: "Miss Garrett, I'm–"

And Toby puked right there on the science room floor.

Miss Garrett pushed the office call button, "Please send a janitor. . ." Then, she said, "Eliot, help Toby to the nurse's office."

I tried to hold my breath. Ironic: dry owl pellets didn't bother me, but puke made me gag. I should have taken off the plastic gloves, but they were comforting. No germs on my hands this way.

"Can you walk?"

Toby nodded, his face a picture of misery. I inched around the mess on the floor and held open the door for Toby.

"Told you I'd win this bet," he mumbled, while staggering down the hall.

"You're crazy. I didn't think you'd go this far just to win a bet."

The nurse's office was already crowded–six other students sitting in chairs or lying on one of the three beds.

"What's going on?" I asked, uneasy.

Miss Clay stuck a digital thermometer in Toby's ear. Beep. "101.5. You've got a temperature, Toby. We'll call your mom to come get you." Then she looked at me. "It's a stomach bug. Too early for the flu. But it's a bad bug; we've already sent home twenty-seven kids today."

A stomach virus or germ or whatever. And I was standing in the middle of the sick room. In the middle of millions, billions, trillions of germs. I didn't need protective gloves; I needed a complete protective body suit.

My throat burned, words barely came out. But I tried to make light of it. "My dad used to say that if he could sell puke on e-Bay for a quarter a bag, he'd be a millionaire."

"Um, bad joke," Miss Clay said, grimacing. "But I've certainly got enough germs flying around this room to last for a long time."

Nothing in the room changed–I understood that. But a sudden terror of flying germs and viruses made my knees weak. I grabbed the back of a chair. But a kid sat there holding his head. I jumped back, my heart pounding in my ears, and I pulled at the plastic gloves, trying to stretch them to cover my arms, too. My feet, I couldn't feel my feet. I stamped hard and finally felt pins and needles and that was better, way better than numb feet.

As if coming from a distance, Miss Clay approached, her mouth moving. But I heard silence.

And then, I started trembling. I shook, shivered like I was cold, from head to foot, and I couldn't make it stop.

Miss Clay was waving kids back and pulled me into a chair; but I sprang up—because the chair was full of germs from kids who had been puking in this room all day long.

I knew I was going crazy; I understood that.

But I couldn't make it stop. I pulled at the glove on my right hand again, pulling so hard that it ripped, and I stared at the hole in the glove and thought of all the germs pouring in to infect my hands. I ripped off the gloves and turned frantically – still shaking so hard it almost hurt – turned in circles, trying to find a sink to wash my hands.

No sink. No water. Just germs, billions and trillions of germs.

I sank into a corner and hid my face in the crook of my elbow.

Soothing hands smoothed back my hair, and slowly I realized that someone was murmuring things: Try to relax. This will pass.

Murmuring: You're fine. Just a little anxiety attack. It'll go away.

Just a little panic and that's OK. It will pass.

Yes, I was crazy; I understood that. Finally, my breathing slowed, and I could peek out. Miss Clay was seated beside me. She smiled, her lips thin. "Feeling better?"

I tried to answer; instead, I started shivering again. But this time, it passed quickly. "Better," I finally breathed.

"We'll call your mom in a little while. Will that be good?"

Then Toby called, "Miss Clay, I'm—"

And then Toby puked again, right there on the floor of the sick room.

And then, the fire alarm went off.

Mr. Benton's voice came over the loud speaker: "This is NOT a drill. I repeat, this is not a drill. Teachers, please follow the fire drill procedures and take your students outside quietly and quickly. This is not a drill."

And I thought: "This is when Miss Clay needs to panic."

But she didn't.

Miss Clay lined up the sick kids and led them to the door. "Each of you buddy up with someone. Eliot, help Toby. He's too weak to walk very well."

Help Toby? But Toby was filthy dirty with germs, and I would catch the flu, for sure.

Toby sat on the bed with his head in his hands, moaning. The room stank of puke, and I stank of fear and sweat, and the fire alarm wailed and wailed and wailed.

But Toby, my best friend, needed me.

I pushed up, suddenly glad to be off the cold floor, and stood in front of Toby. "Let's go."

No response, except more moans.

I gritted my teeth and reached under Toby's arm and heaved. He staggered up and flung an arm across my shoulders. I turned my face away and held my breath, trying not to breathe in germs, and took a step toward the door Miss Clay was holding open. Toby followed my lead and we stumbled toward the door.

"Hurry," Miss Clay urged. "This isn't a drill."

At some point in the next hour, I realized I was totally zoned out. I had no idea what was happening around me. I knew we were outside for a long time, with Toby's feverish body beside me. Slowly, I noticed a few things. Mrs. Zane came and Toby went. Then the firemen called the all clear, and the ladder trucks drove quietly away: some kid in third grade had tried to smoke cigarettes in the boy's bathroom, or at least that's what everyone around me was saying.

Other sick kids left with parents who had come in answer to Miss Clay's phone calls–she paced in front of the sick kids with her cell phone in her hand.

But when it was time to go back inside, I was still there.

I sat beside Miss Clay in the office while she looked up Marj's cell phone number, which I couldn't remember just then. She explained about my anxiety attack. Turning, Miss Clay said, "Her cell phone battery is low, but she's on her way. She'll be here soon. Why don't you just stay here in the office, away from all the, um, other kids?"

I nodded in relief. And found myself sitting in Mr. Benton's office, alone.

I studied the grandfather clock in the corner. 1:30 p.m.

Marj would be here soon, I told myself. I curled up on the couch and listened to the ticking and watched the pendulum swing. Back and forth. Back and forth.

At 2 p.m., I stood, unsteady, and went out to the secretary to ask her to call Marj again.

"No one answers at her office, and Miss Clay said her cell phone is dead," the secretary said. "I'm sure she's coming as fast as she can."

"Please. Just call again. Please."

Shaking her head in sympathy—she must have been told about the panic attack—the secretary dialed again. Finally, she hung up. "She's got to be on her way."

I went back to the ticking and the pendulum until 2:32 p.m., then asked her to call again. Nothing.

The third time, at 3:13 p.m., I whispered, "Maybe she was in a wreck or something. Maybe she's hurt." I drew a shaky breath. "Maybe she fainted."

"No, no. Sometimes parents just get hung up."

"Could you call the hospital? Call the emergency room, the ER?"

"It's OK, Eliot, she's on her way. Why don't you see if you can lie down again?"

Instead, I sat, head in hands, watching the clock inch forward.

Ring! Ring! Ring! 3:30 p.m. School was out.

I stood in the doorway of the principal's office and watched the school empty out. No one came in, everyone went out.

Until, finally, just after the grandfather clock bonged four times, Mr. Benton came back in the building and strolled into the office.

"Oh, Eliot. Hi. Still here?"

"Yes, sir."

"I talked to your mom about an hour ago," he said. "She said she had an emergency, but she'd be here before I left at 5 p.m."

"You talked to her? She's okay? She's not in the ER?"

"No, no. Everything's fine." Mr. Benton slapped my back in encouragement. "Just some car trouble or something. She was calling from a pay phone because her cell phone was dead."

So I sat, waiting, because Miss Clay said I couldn't go home alone. Listened to the grandfather clock chime. Every fifteen minutes. While I waited and waited and waited, I thought about how angry I was right now and how she should have been here three hours ago. Mrs. Zane came right away for Toby. Other parents had checked out kids all day long. But not Marj. No, not Marj. Not, Marjorie Turner Griffith.

Finally at five minutes until five, Marj walked in.

When Marj walked in, I crossed my arms over my chest.

"Eliot, I'm sorry I'm late."

"Yeah."

But Marj didn't pay any attention to me. She was explaining to Mr. Benton what had happened. She had a double flat in a construction zone where the new road was three or four inches above the old road. A car swerved in the other lane, and Marj overcorrected her steering. Her car fell off the lane into the old roadbed, and both tires on that side went flat. Of course, she said, it took an hour to get a tow truck, then a couple more hours to buy new tires and have them put on. And her cell phone was dead, as in not even the car charger would make it work. What a day, she said.

Mr. Benton made comforting noises, but none of it mattered to me. I had tried and tried and tried to be patient, but that was over.

Marj could have, should have, taken a taxi to school and picked me up. Or asked Mrs. Lopez to get me. Anything. Even going home with Alli to Mr. Porter's house would have been better than sitting in the principal's office for half a day.

I gritted my teeth to keep from yelling at her.

She finished explaining, and Mr. Benton let us go. "Watch the news tonight and in the morning. We're talking to health officials about closing school because of this stomach virus. We had 30% absent today."

Finally Marj looked at me. "But that's not what Eliot had?"

"No. Miss Clay explained to you about anxiety attacks?"

"Yes." But Marj sounded uncertain. Then she straightened and said, "We'll get him an appointment tomorrow. Meanwhile, it's been a long, busy day, and I'm starved."

So, she was going to ignore it and act like nothing had happened. We barely spoke on the way home, me sitting on my hands to remind myself to be quiet. Marj drove through the Hot Wings place on the way home, but ordered mild wings, the kind she liked. We ate in silence, the way she liked.

Then, she went into her office and I trudged upstairs and lay on my bed. Fuming. She didn't even ask about my day. Didn't want to hear about my fears.

When she finally came upstairs to say goodnight, I was beyond furious. Beyond caution. Beyond caring if I offended her.

Marj had changed to a black T-shirt and jeans and looked pale. "You okay?"

"No, I'm mad. Why didn't you come and get me?"

She blinked. "Flat tires."

I spoke through gritted teeth, holding my clenched fists still. "Miss Clay told you I had an anxiety attack, and you didn't come for me for three and a half hours. Three. And a half."

"Eliot," Marj said in a reasonable voice, "I couldn't come." She looked puzzled, like she really didn't get it.

"You could have taken a taxi."

"What?"

"If you wanted to come, if you really cared about me, you could have taken a taxi. Or called a friend to get me. Or – " I stopped. Marj's eyebrows flexed up and down and inward as her face reflected her emotional roller coaster: surprise, shock, confusion.

"I didn't know it mattered."

"Matter? You're supposed to be my mom, aren't you? Of course, it matters."

She opened her mouth, and then shut it. And I thought of the adoption papers sitting on her desk, waiting until the Bread Project was finished, waiting until Marj decided.

I thought: This would be the perfect moment for Marj to reach over and give me a hug.

Instead, she shook her head. "We've both had a difficult day. I'm sorry I couldn't make it to the school right away, and I'm sorry you don't understand. I've never been a mother before, and I'm doing the best I can." She raised both palms. "So let's just both calm down and go to sleep, and we'll see where we are in the morning. I'll take the day off, and we'll get you a doctor's appointment and see what he says."

I had been right to give up on her and plan for a future in a foster home, to gather pictures of Griff and to save money. Alli just didn't understand how bad things were between Marj and me. There was nothing to fight for. Because there was nothing there to start with. And when that thought hit me, I wrapped my arms around my own shoulders and my body went limp and I thought, "I'm sleepy."

I yawned. Lying back on my pillow, I turned my head away. "Good night."

"Good night," she whispered. She touched my shoulder lightly, but I didn't turn, and she went downstairs.

The next day, it was a quick trip to the doctor's office.

Dr. Jay asked, "Eliot, how long has it been since you took your anxiety medicine?"

I shivered and slipped my arms back into my shirt and buttoned it up. "Maybe three years." Since I'd met Griff, I guessed.

"Well, we'll just try the same medicine, just a little stronger since you've grown so much." He flipped some pages in my chart and flipped back to the front to scribble. Then he talked to Marj about anxiety attacks and handed her three full-color brochures and a prescription.

I sat there, embarrassed, and pretended it was all about someone else.

Marj's face became more solemn, her lips straighter, her back stiffer. She started drumming her fingers on her knee. Finding out about this problem just made things worse.

When Griff had found out, he was practical. We talked about it several times, and in the early days before Griff adopted me, we made the meds part of our daily routine; and, of course, Griff was in the nurse's office when the panic attacks hit so he was there to help me get through them. And later, after Griff adopted me, the panic attacks went away and we celebrated after a month of no attacks, and again, after two months of no attacks. Somehow, I didn't think Marj would be practical or open or helpful. She wouldn't be there.

Sitting in the examining room, still shivering, my anger flared again. I glared at the framed photo on the wall, a photo of a mother grizzly teaching her cub to fish.

An hour later, Marj dropped me off at the house—school was closed because of the flu—and went to the office. "I just need to finish one file, and I'll be home. What do you want for supper?"

I shrugged, but the habit of trying to please adults was still there. "Supreme pizza." It was her favorite.

Marj frowned. "I thought you liked pepperoni, not supreme."

That made me look up. That simple thing, that she remembered I liked pepperoni pizza, it made me soften. "Either way. Supreme is good, too."

She nodded, and briefly a smile crossed her face. A flash of hope shot through me. Maybe she just needed more time to think.

BREAD PROJECT, WEEK 8

ELIOT

Inside, I called Alli and asked if she wanted some lunch; she came over ten minutes later. Neither of us was hungry yet, so we went upstairs. I sat at the computer and pulled up Griff's webpage and started working on putting in some of the photos I had scanned.

Looking over my shoulder, Alli whistled. "Your mom know about this webpage?"

"Don't call her my mom. And, no. She doesn't. She never asks what I'm doing on the computer. Just assumes I'm playing video games."

Alli whistled again. "Oh. You had an argument with her."

I whirled around my chair and glared. "Do you know how long I had to wait for her to come get me yesterday? Three and a half hours. Forever." My arms were crossed, and I barely kept myself from shaking with anger.

"So, where was she?"

I explained about the flat tires. "I know. It's a good excuse. But it's still an excuse."

"So you blew up. Argued with her."

"No. We just didn't talk."

Alli whistled again, and I thought that if she did that irritating sound one more time, I'd make her leave.

She said, "That's even worse. You didn't compare her to Griff did you?"

"Not out loud."

"Better not ever say that out loud," Alli said. She bent down so her eyes were on the same level with mine, and then paused to make sure I was looking straight at her. "Do that? She'll be very, very, very mad." Her point made, Alli stood straight. "Well, I won't let you give up on her. You're good at writing," – she waved at the computer – "so write her a letter about what happened and why and how you feel. Surprise her. Communicate."

"Maybe." I'd have to wait and see what Marj said later about the new medicine. Oh. I hoped it wasn't expensive medicine.

"Think about it," Alli said. "Meanwhile, we need to talk about the Bread Project. With school closed for the flu, we won't have a Bread Project assembly tomorrow. We need to pass on the starter ourselves."

"Marj said that, too. But then, she had to go to work. How many starters are we talking about?'

"Pick up from 64. Deliver to 64."

For a minute, I had visions of walking around south Nashville for endless hours. Then reality hit: "It's impossible."

"No, I have it all worked out."

Alli pulled a crumpled paper from the pocket of her school uniform—why did she wear that uniform all the time? She explained that she had divided the Project into eight shorter lists and called the committee—Mrs. Lopez and Mrs. Patel and Mrs. Johnson—and assigned each a list. She had even talked to Marj at her office. Then those four women each called two friends until eight mothers were in charge of just eight jars of starter each. They would make sure the sourdough starter got passed to the next person or call the committee person for help. "We might get phone calls, though, to pick up starter to take somewhere. I told everyone to call me or you if they needed a delivery service."

Somewhere along the way, the Bread Project had become important to Alli. She wanted the Project to work, needed the Project to work. Like she really cared about the community. Cared about getting people to work together. I could see that the thrill for her was in the people, how an idea could act like yeast in people's lives and multiply and grow, and make people stick together better.

I wanted the Project to work, too, but for selfish reasons. And for me? It would always be the feel of the dough under my hands and the taste of the bread. Not in the impossible-to-control feelings of others.

Watching her wave her arms around and talk with excitement, I realized something else, too: without Alli, the Bread Project would fall apart. With school cancelled, I would have given up this week. Instead, Alli had divided up the task and handed out jobs. She kept everyone involved. How did she know how to do all that?

❖

"You've got my problems solved and the Bread Project under control," I said. "Let's work on your problem now."

I made Alli write down everything she could remember about her dad: full name, birthday, brothers, sisters, names of friends, and where he served in the Army. She only knew bits and pieces, so she ran to the Porters and brought back an brought an envelope with one photo of her dad and scraps of paper.

Alli explained that there weren't any pictures with her mom. "She died right after I was born. No one thought to make pictures. This one is me and my dad. It's a Wal-Mart portrait taken sometime before I was a year old, because that's when he went overseas. Do you really think he could be alive?"

It was an old photo, and I suddenly felt rich with all the photos of Griff. "It's possible," I said. I tried to be reassuring, but we both knew it was a long shot.

I had typed up what I had. We deleted and changed information until the document had everything on it that she knew. I even scanned the photo so when I needed it, I could upload it to the sites where retired soldiers hung out.

It wasn't enough, I knew that. Not nearly enough. But we'd try, anyway. It would only take one person recognizing one fact here or there to make the connection. And if that happened, we'd find her dad – if he was still alive.

One thing still bothered me: "We can't use our real names and addresses, you know."

"Why not?" Alli said.

"Cyberstalking."

"But you have to use my name, so my dad will know it's really me."

"Yeah, that makes it hard." I had an idea, but I hesitated. This idea would be expensive, and neither of us had much money right now. But I couldn't think of anything else. "We need to rent a post office box. We'll tell people to send a letter to the PO box.

That way, we won't have to use our names. Well, my name, anyway."

Alli paced the floor beside my computer. Then she stopped and said, "You're right. How much?"

"I checked their website. About $50 a year for a small box. That's all we need." I tried to close my mouth and not say anymore, but Alli was shaking her head. So, my mouth opened by itself, "I can pay half."

She smiled at that. "Are you sure?"

I nodded.

"Thanks." It was a small word, but it made me feel big.

We looked through the usps.gov website, trying to figure out the PO boxes. Looked like they'd need an adult signature, but we could forge that. But still, one of us would have to go down there and rent the box.

Finally, we went downstairs and made peanut butter and grape jelly sandwiches. We sat in the bright breakfast room to eat. And to hope.

Alli took a big bite of sandwich and mumbled, "Do you think it will work?"

I unstuck my tongue from the roof of my mouth. "If he's out there, we'll find him."

"What if he doesn't like me? This is scary."

That made me mad. "Scary? Your real Dad can't be scarier than Mr. Porter."

She rolled her eyes and agreed. "I'll get that PO box rented this week. Even if I have to cut school to do it."

Marj ran a hand through her hair and handed me a glass of water and one of those brownish-yellow plastic safety bottles full of pink pills. And then, a glass of water. Didn't speak. Just motioned for me to take a pill.

How much did it cost? I wondered. But didn't have courage to ask.

She watched me take one pill.

Then she sighed, put the medicine bottle in the cabinet, got a drink of water for herself, put the glass in the dishwasher, turned, walked out and disappeared into her office. All without looking at me again.

I waited a few minutes to be sure she was busy. Then, I pulled the package out of the trash. $150. For thirty pills. Five dollars a pill. I searched the package and saw in small print, "Insurance denied. Patient not on this policy."

I wasn't on her health insurance policy because I wasn't officially her son. Before Griff adopted me, the state had insurance for me. After he adopted me, I was supposed to go on his insurance. Now, I guess I was on no one's insurance.

Trembling hands put the package back in the trash.

Trembling legs walked out of the kitchen.

Passing Marj's office, she barely glanced up. The corners of her mouth jerked back into a tight smile. Then rebounded into a straight line.

I trudged upstairs to my room, trembling inside now.

Three weeks from today was the day after Thanksgiving. I didn't have much time left. I had to finish Griff's website. And that's what I did all weekend long, worked on Griff's website.

ALLI

Yeah. I wanted Eliot to look for my dad on the Internet. But I wasted a week, didn't go right away to the post office? Why'd I wait?

Don't know. Really, I don't know. For a couple days, I was just numb, couldn't think. I mean, I'm not Little Orphan Annie, and there aren't really any Daddy Warbucks out there. Did I actually expect to find my dad? No.

So, why try?

Well, why not try? The PO box was the only hard thing. After that, Eliot said it was easy.

All week, I argued back and forth with myself, but didn't make any decisions.

I put Eliot off by saying you had to plan something like cutting school, so there was less chance of getting caught. He kept saying he had it all ready to go. Just waiting on the PO box.

I expected to be busy with the Bread Project that week, going from 128 starters to 256. But the committee had everything under control, Mrs. Lopez said. They had already divided up names and assigned someone to contact the new families. Either call them or visit them. That was a great idea, Mrs. Lopez said.

She didn't realize that now, I felt left out. Mrs. Patel and her helpers were doing the cookbook. Mrs. Johnson was in charge of setting up and decorating for the banquet. Mrs. Lopez was handing out flyers in the community, hoping to get people to come to the bread auction. Mrs. Winston and about six others each had jobs. Only Eliot and I were left out.

It reminded me of Mandy telling me about the new baby about six months ago. We went out on a date, just us two women, she said. Shopping and getting beautiful, she said. Mandy has this really curly hair and likes to make a big deal of getting haircuts, manicures, and then eating at a good restaurant. I loved those days. Even if I wasn't beautiful like Mandy.

"Such soft hair," Frances, the hairdresser, always said to me. "A golden brown. Let's get it trimmed."

She cut some—there was hair on the floor—but it never looked much different to me.

After our haircuts, we stopped at The Brothers Antique Mall, one we had stopped at several times lately. Walking in, you almost felt like it was the game booths from the back-to-school party again. A couple aisles, lots of booths in a giant room. But these booths were packed with old things, things leftover from a lifetime of living, Ted said when he went with us.

Some booths were interesting. Old Barbie dolls, old quilts, old Matchbox cars or action figures. Old. Everything was old. At the booths with glassware, I held my hands behind my back, so the sales clerks didn't get nervous that I'd break something. Some people were sure proud of their junk.

Mandy sorta floated along, her spring dress loose and flowing. Usually, she strolled slowly, looking at every booth. This time, she looked with me at the Barbie dolls. Often, we got one of the dolls or sometimes just a $1 action figure. Today, I was hoping for the Wedding Barbie. It was expensive, but I'd been looking at it every time we came here.

This time, she ignored the other booths and headed toward the back of the mall. She stopped in front of a booth with furniture. A long table with carved legs and matching carved chairs. An old organ. With a sideways look, she stepped into the booth and stood right behind the organ. "Come and see."

It was a small doll cradle, golden colored like my hair. I touched it, and it rocked. No squeaks, just a smooth rock. Excited, I thought, this would be perfect for my dolls.

I picked up the price tag. "500 dollars?" I was shocked.

Mandy smiled, her face lighting up. "I know it's expensive, but Ted insisted. Said if I liked it, we should get it."

"That's too much." But I stroked the golden wood. It was easy to see why she liked it. "Just to put my dolls in, it costs too much."

"Oh." Mandy knelt now, till she was eye level. "It's not for your dolls. We're going to have a baby." Her hand went to her stomach, holding in the flowery dress, protective already. "Isn't it exciting?"

She stood and kept chattering. "We just found out that the baby will come about Thanksgiving time. I'm hoping for a girl with curly hair." She touched the cradle and it rocked again, smooth and easy, with just a finger keeping it going.

Baby. We were having a baby. I knew Ted and Mandy had wanted a baby for a long, long time, and now – this was exciting! I flung my arms around Mandy's waist, full of joy.

She took a sharp breath, unloosed my arms and stepped back. "Oh, not so wild. I'll have to be very careful for the next six months. Till the baby comes." She leaned over and gave me a small hug.

I stammered, "Oh, I'm sorry. I'm sorry. Are you okay?"

"Fine." She turned back to the cradle. "I'm going to get it. Right now. We'll take it home together, put it in the guest room and start turning that room into a nursery. Okay?"

Tears filled my eyes. I was so happy that Mandy was happy. "Yes!"

"Is there anything you want?"

"I want you to name her Emily."

"Why?" Mandy laughed.

"I don't know. I just like that name. Say it: Emily Payne. Doesn't it sound great?"

"We'll see what Ted says. Is there anything you want from the booths here?"

I did want the Wedding Barbie, but not today. Today, it should be something special for Emily. "Can I look a little more?"

"Sure. I'll just ask them to take the cradle to the front of the store."

I wandered the aisles, stopping and looking, but nothing seemed right. I wanted to get something for the baby, something special. Then I saw it. An old quilt. It was red and white, with school houses on it. Small. A baby quilt. Just perfect. Soft and gentle and perfect for the curly-haired baby girl. My sister.

I carried the quilt to the front, and when Mandy saw it, she sat down on a chair and pulled me close, one arm around my shoulder, the other hand on her belly. "Thank you, Alli. This is really special."

Later Ted joined us for lunch. "We are excited," he said, "but we want you to stay. You'll be a big sister."

But even then, it felt different. I'd lived with them for five years and they still hadn't adopted me. With the baby coming, I wasn't sure if they still wanted me. Was Ted just saying that about being a big sister, or did he mean it?

The Bread Project didn't need me any more either. So, I could do whatever I needed to see Baby, and then I didn't care if Miss Brodie-Rock moved me a thousand miles away. I was a big sister, and I would see Baby.

BREAD PROJECT, WEEK 9

ALLI

So, the next week, I did it. On Monday. Right before lunch, I cut school and raced to the post office.

Right off, I saw that sparrow. I just stepped into the post office, and there it was. Pecking, trying to eat something from off the tile floor.

Weird, I thought. Just plain weird.

It was Monday, about noon, just fifteen days before the Thanksgiving banquet, or seventeen days until Thanksgiving itself. Maybe the sparrow was coming inside to get out of the cold. This weekend had turned off really cold. Close to freezing.

I took another step, and the sparrow got scared. Flew up to the top of the two-story tall room and sat on a windowsill. How long had it been trapped in here? No food, no water. How did it survive?

Because survival is what life is all about, isn't it?

I made sure the money was still in my pocket. Last week, my fingers poked through the pockets on this school uniform. Miss Porter sewed it back up, but I didn't trust her sewing. Not with that ancient Singer machine.

Yep, the money was still there, a fat wad of bills wrapped with a rubber band.

This lady came out of the next set of doors. I was looking at that sparrow, so I forgot I was supposed to be invisible; she saw me, all right. Turned around and stared at me as I walked past. It was the school uniform, of course. But I had a good story to tell. No one would question it.

I pushed open the first set of double doors. All along the walls were tiny golden brass doors numbered from 1 to—I walked around the corner to see the last number—1 to 500. Floor to ceiling, 500 post office boxes; 500 people getting their mail delivered right there in those boxes. What a sight.

A fat, sweaty man came in, and I drew back, making myself small. I was good at that. I could do it so fast and so good that people just looked through me. Later they'd swear I wasn't even there.

The fat man hitched up his pants. He bent over, his belt cutting his belly in half. Bleh. He fitted a key into a post office box door and pulled out some envelopes. With a grunt, he stood back up, hitched up his pants, and left, without even glancing at me.

Looking at the 500 boxes, I thought: hope we don't get one on top, 'cause I won't be able to reach it.

My stomach was thundering up a storm. Ignoring it, I pushed through the next doors and joined the waiting line. Right in front of me, a bottle-blond lady held a box of envelopes.

"Next." The clerk sounded like a drill sergeant. He had a five-o'clock shadow, buzz haircut and Army-insignia tattoos on his forearms.

The lady said, "These are invitations to a baby shower. Do you have any stamps with babies on them?"

The clerk opened a drawer, flipped things around, and then tossed something at the lady. "Look at these," he ordered. "Baby Jesus and Mother Mary."

"Perfect," the lady said. "I'll take 100."

Mother and son, that was nice since it was baby invitations.

"Next."

The woman was at the counter, peeling off baby Jesus stamps and sticking them on her envelopes. My turn.

"Morning." Control that voice, I thought. "My dad, he's in the car sick. Got the flu, you know. But he's got to get a post office box rented today, or his boss will kill him. But then, he's going home and going to bed. Well, anyway, my dad –he's running a temperature, really– said I should come in and give you this stuff." I laid the post office box application and the wad of cash on the counter. My heart was doing such a loud tlot-tlot, trotting so fast that the clerk had to hear it.

The bottle-blond said, "I'm glad he stayed in the car. I don't want to get sick."

The clerk blinked at her, then at me, and then picked up the application.

Eliot had signed it real big. "Like John Hancock," Eliot had said.

"What?"

"You know. The guy who signed the Constitution."

"Oh. Yeah."

Well, anyway, Eliot had signed it real big, and you couldn't read it. That was OK, though, 'cause you can't read most adult's signatures.

The clerk ran his fat finger down the application and nodded once, twice, thrice. Eliot must have done it right, 'cause the clerk picked up the money and counted. It's weird how some people have to straighten up bills when they count. He turned every bill so the guys' heads were facing the same way.

"Only $49. I need $50."

"No," I insisted, "It's $50."

He counted again, faster this time, since the bills were already straightened up. "$49."

How stupid! I should have counted it twice this morning, to make sure. Of course, there was no Dad waiting around outside to give me another dollar. My stomach cramped even harder, this time 'cause I was so mad. Everything was unraveling. No post office box, no posting on the Internet, no Dad.

"Here."

I spun around. A natural-blond guy held out a dollar bill. He had on dress pants, white shirt and tie, but just a jeans jacket. I shivered, realizing I was alone. I stepped back.

"Here," he said again. "I don't want to get the flu from your Dad, and I'm in a hurry. Just the kindness of a stranger, nothing more."

"Take it," the clerk ordered. "How many keys do you need?"

I obeyed. I grabbed the dollar, spun and handed it to the clerk. "There. Dad said two keys." I hoped it was OK to take the man's money. It was in front of the clerk and that lady. And the mail clerk practically ordered me to take it. And I'd never see the blond again. I kept my back straight and didn't look around at the blond guy again.

The clerk handed me a receipt and a handful of other stuff. "Box number 491."

"Is that a high one or a low one?"

He shrugged. "Don't know. Have your dad read the stuff, and if he doesn't like the box number, he can change it later when he feels better."

"Thanks."

I walked out, but I heard the blond man talking to the clerk, "I need stamps for wedding invitations. My fiancé asked for something with hearts."

People sure were picky about stamps.

I stopped and checked the boxes. 491 was eye-height. Perfect. I grinned, thinking, the next time I looked in this box, I might see a letter from my Dad. That sounded magical.

Leaving, I looked for that sparrow again, but he was gone. I hoped he wasn't just hiding; I hoped he was already outside flying around in the big blue sky of that fall day.

Me? After renting the PO box, I felt like I was flying high all afternoon. Barely paid attention in class.

After the last bell, I had to choose. Help Miss Garrett clean the science classroom, especially the fish tanks. Or, sit in Mr. Porter's room and do homework. Sometimes I walked home alone, but lately Mr. Porter wanted me to stay at school and finish homework, so I rode home with him. Science room or Mr. Porter's room? Not a choice, really—I headed for the science classroom.

Walking down the south hallway, the sun streaming in, I was happy. Daydreaming.

Dreaming in broad daylight, warm daylight, glorious daylight. I stopped and leaned against the window that overlooked the back parking lot. And let myself dream like I hadn't dreamed in years.

My dad was waiting in his car, waiting for me to come out. He'd give me a peck on the cheek. I'd give him a hug. Then ask, every so sweetly, if he could stop by the Ice Cream Shoppe on the way home, and of course, he'd say yes, and we'd stop and I'd get a chocolate shake and he'd get a strawberry one. Did Dad like strawberry? Somehow, I just seemed to know that he did. Of course, he did.

Suddenly, I froze, the daydream evaporating. There in the back parking lot, getting out of a car, was a blond man in jeans and white shirt. He'd taken off the tie and left the jeans jacket somewhere, but it was Blondie, the man from the post office. Here!

If he saw me, he'd tell the office that I cut school at lunch. Eventually, I'd be in trouble.

Why was he here?

I darted down the hallway and ducked into the library doorway. Peeked out. The door to the parking lot opened and he stepped inside. Blinked, coming from the bright day to the darker hallway.

Blondie looked undecided, but then turned and walked toward me.

I stepped inside the library and closed the door.

"Can I help you?" asked Mrs. Mac, the librarian. She was four foot eight inches tall, just a midget, she always said. But she knew everything about books and which ones you might like to read.

"Uh, no. I just—" I looked around wildly, trying to find some excuse to be there.

"I see." She cocked her head to the side and looked mischievous. "Trying to avoid going to Mr. Porter's room to do homework right away?"

I nodded in relief. "Could I check out a book first?"

"Sure." Mrs. Mac went back to a cart of returned books and resumed shelving. To reach the top two shelves, she dragged a stool, screeching it across the tile floor.

I pretended to look at books, but finally gave up and just grabbed one and checked it out at the self-service computer. Where had Blondie gone, and why was he here, at the school? Better not take any chances: I'd hide out in Mr. Porter's room. No one ever came to see him.

With the library book, I rushed to my locker and wrestled out my backpack. At every classroom door, I hesitated. Afraid. Was Blondie in this room? Would he see me if I walked by?

I ducked my head and let my hair hide my face. Not that it was enough to stop the man from recognizing me. But it made me feel better.

Finally, I reached Mr. P's room.

As usual, he was putting. Back of the room, he had a green carpet, a putting green, he called it. Kept a set of golf clubs in his back closet. Sometimes, when you finished homework early, he let a student putt. Not often, but sometimes. Didn't like the fingerprints all over his clubs.

He would putt—relax, unwind—for ten or fifteen minutes. Then spend another 30 minutes grading papers or entering grades into the computer.

Quickly, I did my homework. Then looked at the library book. Oh, great. A book on cyber-safety. Of course, I had been standing by the non-fiction books and just grabbed something from the new bookshelf. I flipped through and realized that Eliot had been right about the PO box. We really did need to be careful about the online stuff.

Knock! Knock! Without waiting, the door to the hallway opened.

Startled, I looked up, just as Mr. P stood, scowl on his face.

"Mr. Porter, I want you to meet my fiancé, Shane Baxter." It was Miss Garrett, chattering on, "I've got ten more minutes of work and he's bored, and I wondered if he could use your putting green for a bit until I'm ready to leave? He's really good at golf; maybe you can chat about local golf courses or something. Or, if you're busy, he could just putt by himself."

I stared, horrified. Her fiancé, Mr. Baxter, was Blondie.

As soon as Miss Garrett and Mr. Baxter entered, I covered my eyes with my hand, afraid of being recognized. Didn't help.

"Hey!" Mr. Baxter said. "Weren't you in the post office at lunch?"

Trouble had found me.

Of course, Mr. Porter asked for more information.

"No," he told Mr. Porter, "I didn't hear exactly what she was asking the clerk. I don't know why she was there." He shrugged, like that was the end of it. Looking around, Mr. Baxter asked, "Wow, is that a real knight's armor, or just a reproduction? You say you teach social studies?"

But Mr. Porter's face was red and blotchy with anger. His hands clenched, a sign of building pressure. "Mr. Baxter, do you mind? I'm sorry, Miss Garrett. I need to talk to Alli and find out why she was at the post office. Would you excuse us, please?" He ushered them both back into the hallway and firmly shut the door.

"I'll need an explanation. Now," he demanded.

Here's the thing: Mr. Porter couldn't stand it that I refused to answer his questions. Refused. I declined, I demurred, I eschewed. (Those are good spelling words: decline, demur, eschew.)

I said, "No."

Mr. Porter glared. Asked me again why I went to the post office.

I said, "I can't tell you that."

Mr. Porter asked why I cut school.

"I'm sorry," I said, "I can't answer that." And truly, I was sorry. I knew I was in big trouble. But I was defiant anyway.

Finally, Mr. Porter stopped asking me anything. He sat at his desk for a minute, then got up and went to the back of the room and started putting. Thwack. Thwack. I guess it helped him think or something.

Now that's when fear really struck, and I started trembling. I wasn't fooled. This fight wasn't over, it was just starting. And Mr. Porter held all the aces.

ALLI

Mr. Porter was reasonable and calm. Too calm.

On the way home, he stopped at the barbeque place and picked up some sandwiches. He spoke to me only when he had to: "You want milk or juice?"

I worried about his calmness, even while I tried to imitate his calm voice. "Milk," I said. "Please."

He poured a glass and set it beside my plate. We ate in silence. Then, he said, "Go upstairs now. Finish your homework."

"Yes, sir."

Don't know what Mr. Porter was planning, but something. My guess? He'd probably call Miss Brodie-Rock in the morning. I didn't expect to be here much longer. That meant I needed to find out about Mandy's baby. I needed an Internet connection. Every time I went to Eliot's house, I checked Ted's blog. His last post said that Baby could come any day now. But I was sure Mr. Porter wouldn't let me on the Internet tonight.

I went downstairs to watch TV, but stopped at the guest half-bathroom, the one Miss Porter liked to use. For me, cold weather like this weekend meant chapped hands.

The half-bath was most definitely a room Miss Porter decorated. It had pink and green towels, rosebud colors. I found hand lotion in a drawer, squeezed the tube and coated my hands. They were already red all over. On the right hand, the ring finger and pinkie had cracks on the joints. Had to remember to put on lotion every day. Or they could get worse.

Then, I heard heels clipping down the hall. Coming out of the bathroom, I almost ran into Miss Porter. No skirt, too cold for that. But a rich purple pant suit, probably wool. High heel black boots. And a scarf around her neck. She always dressed so nice for her country club job. She had her cell phone in one hand and ear muffs in the other. "Oh, hello," she said. "Excuse me." She went into the guest bath.

Came out holding the hand lotion and her earmuffs. "You use this?" she asked.

Uh-oh. I had forgotten to put it back in the drawer. I nodded. Waited. Was I in even more trouble?

"Let's see your hands."

Trying not to tremble, I held them out.

She frowned and drew back. "Here." She shoved the almost empty tube at me, then strode past me to the living room. I followed.

"Brother," she said, "Are you going to the grocery store any time soon?"

He sat in his easy chair watching a police detective show. At her question, he looked up. "Sometime."

What was she up to?

"Well, this child needs some hand lotion." She pulled me forward and stuck my hands in front of his face and pointed to the cracked joints. Then she pushed away my hands, took the lotion from me and held it in front of his face. "This is the brand to buy."

I was amazed. Miss Porter sticking up for me, trying to get her brother to do something.

Mr. Porter looked at it carefully. Then shoved it away.

Miss Porter had a hand on her hip. "You know, some people just shouldn't be foster parents. They don't pay enough attention to the child."

Shocked, I thought about what she said, and she was right. Some people might think they'd be good foster parents, till they tried.

Mr. Porter turned up the volume on the TV.

Miss Porter sighed. "Well, I'm going out. Don't wait up."

Embarrassed by Miss Porter's comments, I moved to the window and watched her leave. It was cold, cold, cold. She put on her earmuffs and wrapped up in her scarf. Her car pulled away, the exhaust puffing in the cool air. I had to decide if I would try to stay here until after Baby, or just give up now and let them move me.

I sat on a straight back chair beside the window and watched the profile of Mr. Porter. The lamp's bright light sent deep shadows over half of Mr. Porter's face, accenting his frown lines. He was deeply unhappy. He kept changing channels, watching a few seconds, then flipping to a new channel.

It was true that some people were just not supposed to be foster parents.

But I still had the problem of finding out about Baby, and that would be so much harder if I moved. So, I had to give Mr. Porter something to keep him happy.

I cleared my throat and said loudly, "I went to the post office to mail a card to Mandy and Ted. Congratulations on the baby." It was a good lie, related to what I was worried about so he would believe it, but not the whole truth, either. No way would I ever tell Mr. Porter about the PO box.

Mr. Porter shifted to look at me, then flicked off the TV. "You know, of course, that you're not supposed to contact them."

I shrugged, afraid he'd see it was a lie.

He let out a huge sigh and seemed to sag, as if his backbone had become jelly. "Okay. Thanks for telling me. You'll have to talk to Mr. Benton about cutting school tomorrow and take the consequences. But I won't make the phone call that I thought I had to make. Next time you do something like this, though—" He turned back to the TV and flipped it back on.

"—you'll call Miss Brodie-Rock, and I'll have to move to a new house. Right?" Anger flooded through me. I had guessed right. Well, after I saw Baby, he could do whatever he wanted, and I wouldn't care.

BREAD PROJECT, WEEK 10

ELIOT

That Friday was the last Bread Assembly. Next week was Thanksgiving.

The auditorium looked and sounded different. On the left were seated the kids who already had the sourdough starter, the Haves. Quiet and solemn.

On the right were seated the Have-Nots. Creaky seats. Jokes. Laughter. And a touch of anger at being left out of everything until the last minute, not getting their sourdough starter until just ten days before Thanksgiving.

I held my plastic jar of sourdough starter carefully in my lap. Some kids set their jars on the ground or stuffed them onto the seat beside them. My fingers crept to the lid, itching to tap, to drum. But today was too special. I didn't want to start something like that. The chair creaking had been necessary to distract kids from spitballs. Today, the air was already crackling with excitement, even if kids didn't understand why.

The kindergartners were still down in front, going back to the sixth grade under the balcony. There was a vacant row in the middle, marking the change from the Haves to the Have-Nots. Teachers directed the Sixth, Fifth, Fourth, and Third Grade-Haves to the stairs on the left of the auditorium and the Third, Second, First and Kindergarten Have-Nots to the stairs on the right.

At a signal from Mr. Benton, one row from each section stood and marched forward. My heart thumped, just watching. So many hours had gone into this moment.

The columns met in the center of the stage. The Haves gave the Have-Nots a jar of starter, shook hands and then together, they carefully climbed down the center stairs. At the bottom, each row turned back to seats. From my seat in the back, it all looked like a figure eight circling up and around and back down.

Then two more rows stood and repeated the process. And so on. Back through the rows until it reached my row, and I stood. The line surged forward, then inched along, until I carefully watched my feet and climbed the steps to the stage. There was a steady drumming of feet marching across the stage, but it was the right sound track for this last Bread Assembly.

Finally, I handed the jar of sourdough to a curly haired kindergarten girl. All around us was the smell of sourdough starter, that sharp, yeasty smell.

I whispered, "Take good care of it."

She nodded, solemn.

We marched back to our seats, and finally, everyone in the school had a jar of sourdough starter. When the last kid sat, the adults on stage—Marj, Mr. Benton, Mr. and Mrs. Lopez, Mr. and Mrs. Patel and Mrs. Johnson—broke into smiles and started clapping.

From two rows in front of me, Alli turned and smiled, too. "We did it," she mouthed.

I remembered the first time I saw Alli, so scrawny, and I remembered wincing at her voice, so harsh. Now, I hardly noticed. Oh, she was still scrawny and her voice still harsh. Now, though, I thought of her knocking on the Patel's door and asking for Mrs. Patel's naan recipe. Or at the Zane's house, filling up a pita with meatballs. Or playing cards. Or—

I almost blushed at my thoughts. She wasn't my girlfriend or anything like that! No way.

But she had helped change this community, had gotten them out of their rut. And the strangest: people weren't saying this was Marj's project, or Alli's project, or even Griff's project. Instead, they said, "Our project."

We did it. They did it. Everyone had brought back sourdough starter, and together, they hadn't let anyone set off a chain reaction of failure. They did it.

I sat up straight. Banged my elbows on the seat, but barely noticed. Instead, I was caught by surprise. I had gotten so involved with the weekly struggle. Make sure the sourdough survived the week. Make sure the parents—Mexicans, Kurds, Italians, blacks, whites, Indians, whatever culture – understood the project. Make sure the jars were ready to bring back. Even with Alli dividing up the tasks there were days when we had to go and pick up or deliver starter. The struggle to make it work. The struggle to work together.

And now it had worked. We, all of us, were done. Everyone had a jar of sourdough starter.

I closed my eyes against the tears of release that threatened to fall. Griff would have been proud.

Of course, we still had problems.

I opened my eyes as Mrs. Patel took the microphone and explained. "We had planned to hand out a sourdough cookbook today. But the stomach virus that closed the school last week put us behind, and the cookbooks won't be in until next week. Instead, we are mailing a couple easy recipes to each parent today. Your parents should get the letters tomorrow. Okay?"

Silence.

From behind Mrs. Patel, Marj stood and walked to the microphone. "You did it!" Her quiet but intense voice caught the kids' attention more than a yell would have done. Still without yelling, she said solemnly, "Hurray for bread! Hurray for new playground equipment!" Startled, I realized that Marj was proud. She was proud of the kids, proud of this community that Griff had loved so much, proud that we had made it.

Everyone was silent a moment longer, then the crowd broke out in cheers.

Beside me, Toby grinned. "Everyone has a jar of sourdough starter. But you haven't won that bet until everyone bakes bread and brings it to the Thanksgiving party. 500 loaves, you win. 499, you lose."

And I closed my eyes again, this time from tears of frustration. Toby was right. The Bread Project was only halfway finished.

ALLI

After the Bread Assembly, I ducked into the library and sat at the computer that had Internet access. The librarian would show up any minute, so I typed fast and read Ted's update on BabyPayne.com:

> No change. We're packed and ready to go to the hospital. Any minute.
>
> I'm going to the office at strange times this week, finishing up a big project. It's the last big project before Baby comes.

I sighed. No Baby yet. I still had to make it a couple more days.

ELIOT

After the Bread Assembly, I thought about it all morning: Marj was proud of what we had done. She had told Mrs. Lopez that she'd never done something like this, could never have made it work. But Marj didn't have to do it all alone: the community came together, the community made it work. Toby might be right that only 499 loaves would show up at the Thanksgiving dinner next week, but we'd already done a lot.

It all made me ache somewhere deep inside. Things were getting better, and maybe this space of time, these few months, had given Marj and me a chance to become a family. I felt the craving even deeper than before. Maybe because—in spite of everything—I liked Marj. How she had refused to give up. How she was sad and yet didn't stop trying and working hard. I wanted us to be a real family. But I had no idea what her decision would be.

Later that day in science class, we studied microbes.

"Think about everything happening at school for the last week," Miss Garrett said. "We had a stomach virus. Microbes. And today, we finished handing out the sourdough starter. Microbes."

I knew this class was going to be bad for me. Of course, Miss Garrett was right. Viruses caused the flu, and we needed to study that. And a combination of yeast and bacteria created the sourdough starter: the yeast gave off the carbon dioxide gas to make the bread rise and the bacteria made the pH levels acidic, giving it that sour taste. All good science. But I hadn't thought of either as microbes.

That name: microbes. Mike-Robes. Like a scruffy man wearing a bath robe. But it was more sinister than that. It was like the "Robes" part was a soft fluffy thing that could envelope you and smother you. And "Mike" ended with that hard K sound, like it had just stabbed you. Stabbed and wrapped in softness that smothered you. Microbes.

Miss Garrett handed me a set of glass slides. Then leaned over and whispered. "You okay?"

She knew about the panic attacks, all the teachers did. I glanced at Marissa and the other girls. Blushed. "Of course!" I snapped.

Miss Garrett hesitated. But then said, "If you need to, you know, go out of the room or something, just raise your hand."

I turned away, really embarrassed now. Put the first slide under our microscope, then motioned for Marissa to look first. 'Cause I was scared to look. In fact, I was starting to feel bad. My face was hot. My breath was quicker.

I took a deep breath and tried to force myself to breathe slow and deep. I needed to make sure Mike-Robes didn't attack.

Marissa had her dark hair in one long braid; better for softball she had just told one of the other girls. But curls escaped the braid and wisped around her face. I concentrated on the curls.

Don't think of Mike-Robes. Look at the curls.

Marissa had to brush them out of her way three times before she could focus the microscope. I tried to smile, tried to be amused.

Marissa mumbled, talking to herself almost, hard to hear because of the microscope. Said something about, "There could be millions of these things in a drop of water, and we wouldn't even know."

Millions. Or billions.

Marissa straightened up and let the next girl look.

At the front, Miss Garrett had a special microscope that projected onto a white board so she could talk and point out things for us to look for. "Your second slide has a drop of the sourdough starter. You'll see two different shapes: yeast and bacteria – that's what makes it work."

Millions of yeast. Billions of bacteria.

I could hear Marj's triumphant voice: "Hurray for bread! Playground equipment!"

But her voice was faint. Smothered.

The world whirled around me. Then, ashamed that I was so weak, I raised my hand.

Miss Garrett's face paled. She nodded, not waiting for me to speak.

Instantly, I was up and racing out the door and toward the nurse's office.

But when I got there, I couldn't step inside. I stopped in the doorway. Miss Clay was swabbing a kid's arm with gauze. A girl. Small, probably second grade. Scraped elbow. The gauze all bloody. Oh!

Miss Clay's voice was sharp. "Eliot! Are you okay?"

I leaned over and held on to my knees and breathed deep. Deeper. Slower. And somehow—somehow—I didn't slip into the panic. I still felt shaky, but I was holding it together. Maybe.

I straightened and nodded. But then the sight of the blood made me dizzy again.

"Don't look over here. Sit at the other desk."

I obeyed.

No, really. I obeyed. I was in control, and I could do what someone told me. I could hear Miss Clay, and I could sit at the desk and not look at something that might make me feel worse.

"I'm okay," I said.

"What?" Miss Clay sounded worried. "I'm almost finished here."

"I'm okay." I said with surprise. "I'm really okay."

Later, when the kid's arm was bandaged, and she was sent back to class, Miss Clay laid a hand on my shoulder, and I spun my chair around. And smiled. "I'm okay."

She bent and looked at my eyes and held my wrist and took my pulse.

Then she smiled. "You are okay."

And suddenly, I wanted Marj to know. "Can I call my mom and tell her that I'm okay? That I almost panicked, but I didn't. I'm okay."

"I think that's a fabulous idea."

While I sat at her desk and dialed Marj's number, Miss Clay stepped outside to the hallway.

"Hello. Marj Winston's office." It was Marj's secretary.

"Oh, hi, Miss Street. This is Eliot. Can I talk to Marj?" Heart full of joy, I could hardly get out the words.

"Sorry, she's just left."

"Oh." The bubble of joy burst. But that was OK. I could just tell her later. Maybe call back later or call her cell phone. "Do you think she'll be back soon?"

There was a pause. "Let's see. She had to stop by the courthouse and talk to a social worker. Then stop by to see a Mr. Donovan."

"Oh." She was going to see a social worker. And Mr. Donovan was the adoption lawyer. And a wave of tiredness swept over me. I just wanted to sleep. "Oh."

"Do you want to leave a message for your mom, Eliot?"

"No. No message."

No message. Because there was no mom.

ALLI

Friday night, it was strange, but both Miss Porter and Mr. Porter were home, playing Scrabble in the living room. Didn't invite me to play, though. It was a running feud between them. Over the years, Mr. Porter had won 430 times to Miss Porter's 417 times.

I glanced over her shoulder and realized she'd misspelled "asault." (Assault. A sudden, violent attack. Origin: French. A-s-s-a-u-l-t. The double-s is what made this a hard word.)

They only let me play Scrabble twice.

"Alli, you're a professional speller," Mr. Porter had said. "It wouldn't be fair."

I didn't tell him now about Miss Porter's mistake. And while their attention was on shuffling wooden letters around, I quietly sat at the computer desk in the living room and pulled up the Baby Payne blog:

Yes! We're on the way to the hospital. Baby is coming tonight or early tomorrow morning. Pics as soon as I can.

Ted, the new father-to-be.

Oh. I caught my breath.

Then quickly looked to see if the Porters had noticed. But they were still busy with Scrabble. Ted had posted that message at three that afternoon. Baby could already be here!

So. Tonight was the night. My heart pounded with excitement, and I was afraid they'd hear even that.

Finally, I went upstairs and pretended to sleep. It was eleven before the Scrabble game finished, and Miss Porter peeked in my room to make sure I was asleep. It was midnight, before I slipped my feet out the window and sat on the sill of the second floor of the historic home that the Porters called home. Stepped to the tree limb and dropped lower. Lower. To the ground.

I sat with my back against the tree trunk, knees pulled up, trying to stay warm. For a while, I just sat, not thinking, just watching the moonlight flicker through the leaves. Smiling. But it was cold. I stood and hoisted my backpack and started walking.

I had everything in my pack that I wanted from the Porter's house. Left the school uniforms and schoolbooks. Just took my street clothes, my red picture album, my few books and my stash of $78. I knew that I wouldn't be back, that this would end with Miss Brodie-Rock. But I was going to the hospital to see Baby! My sister.

ELIOT

I was in the breakfast room, crunching corn flakes and reading cartoons in the morning newspaper when the phone rang.

In the kitchen, I heard Marj answer, "'Lo."

A moment later, she sat beside me, holding her hand over the phone. "It's Mr. Porter. Alli's run away. Her bed wasn't slept in. You know where she is?"

Baby, I thought. Of course, that was it. "No," I said, my eyes wide, trying to look innocent.

Marj repeated that to Mr. Porter, then clicked off the portable phone and sat with her hands in her lap, just watching me.

I shrugged.

"Well?" she said.

"The hospital. Mandy and Ted Payne must be having their baby."

"How would Alli know that?"

"BabyPayne.com"

Marj sighed. Then she shook her head and sighed again. "Mr. Porter has already called the social worker. They are looking for her and I don't know–" she hesitated.

"Mr. Porter doesn't want her to stay there any longer. Alli knows."

Marj's brow furrowed. "And she still did this?"

How to explain Alli's obsession with the baby? Her fears about that fall Mandy had taken, how she blamed herself? How she wanted to see her sister?

I'd been listening to it for weeks and still didn't quite get it. Didn't matter, Alli got it.

Marj held up the phone.

"No," I said. "Please. Let's go to the hospital and make sure she's there. If she is, then you can call and tell Mr. Porter. But let's find her first. That way, she won't be alone when the social worker comes for her."

Marj studied me. "You've been expecting this."

My throat was tight, afraid she might not understand. I could only nod.

Sunlight flashed through a prism hung in the window, splashing rainbows across Marj's face. She blinked at the light. "It's important to you?"

"Yes."

"Okay. Get dressed, and we'll go. Hurry."

"Thanks," I said, relief flooding through me.

Alli wasn't sorry for what she had done, and I wasn't sorry for her, either. That her actions today would cause her to change foster homes and change schools–it didn't matter as much as what she was doing. Every child deserves to have a special welcome into this cruel world. And Alli would welcome the Payne baby as only a big sister can celebrate the arrival of a little sister. Even if the joy only lasted a moment, it was important, this celebration of kinship.

I gave Marj a fast hug, grabbed my breakfast bowl and practically threw it into the sink before I took the stairs two at a time.

Because after the celebration, Alli might need the support of an old friend.

ALLI

I got to the hospital about 2 a.m. and easily followed the signs to the Labor and Delivery floor. Two other families sprawled all over the waiting room, talking, playing cards. The nurses thought I belonged to one of them. I couldn't ask about Mandy's delivery and how it was going. All I could do was check the nursery every thirty minutes or so. Finally, about 4 am, I pushed two of the hard chairs together and lay curled up. I woke to find a red blanket over me. It wasn't dark there; the hallway lights were still on, though, dimmed. The large wall clock said 6:30 a.m.

I got up, blanket still wrapped around my shoulders like a cape with just socks on my feet, and walked around the corner to the nursery to study the rows of babies.

I knocked softly on the glass. Thick. It ran about the length of a school bus. Beyond it clustered bassinets (Bassinet: a basket used as a baby's cradle. Origin: French. B-a-s-s-i-n-e-t. Another double-s word.) Maybe a dozen bassinets. Babies were wrapped up like little burritos, the blankets wound around them until it was impossible for them to move. Only small faces shone out. Some babies cried while others lay quietly, dark eyes looking around. Most slept, with pacifiers trapped in their mouths by the burrito wrapping.

I was most interested in the cards taped to each bassinet, the baby's last names. They weren't lined up in alphabetical order or anything. Just had to look through all of them. Looking for Payne.

But she wasn't there.

A pregnant woman, her belly big like a giant egg, passed and thinking about Mandy's belly, I had to ask, "When will your baby come?"

She wore a nightgown and robe and walked with a wobble, while one hand pushed on her back. "I'm in labor, now. Just walking to speed things up," she said. "You a big sister? Which one is yours?"

"She's not there yet."

"Be patient. Babies don't wait long."

And then I heard Ted. He was in the doorway of the nursery, talking to a nurse, a short woman with salt-and-pepper hair worn in a ponytail.

"We're in room 226," Ted said. "I've got to run home and get a few things. I'll be back in an hour. My mother-in-law is asleep, but so is the baby. That's okay, right?"

So that's where the baby was, in the room with Mandy.

"I can bring her back to the nursery if you want," the nurse said. "But she's okay in the room, as long as there's another adult there."

"Great, I'll be back soon," Ted said.

I stepped toward the window, hoping the pregnant woman would shield me from Ted's view. And somehow, he didn't see me, just walked past, got on the elevator and disappeared. This was my chance: I would slip into the room, see Baby and leave. By the time Ted got back, I'd be gone, too.

ELIOT

Just as you walk in the hospital, there is a waiting room. That was the worst. I hadn't been back to the hospital since Griff died, and what I remembered the most was that empty, boring waiting room. The blue and red striped sofa was still there. That was where I sat, not sleeping or eating or speaking or anything while Griff slipped away from us. The red blankets, the smell of burned coffee, the complaints of relatives who just wanted a smoke but had to go outside–it all felt familiar. And awful.

I was glad we rushed past to the elevators and pushed the button for the Labor and Delivery floor. Getting on, a man got off; I turned and watched him until the elevator doors closed. Then, I tugged at Marj's arm. "I think that man was Ted Payne. I've seen his picture on the baby blog."

She whirled around and stared at the closed elevator doors. "We'll just ask what room the Paynes are in and see if we can talk to Mrs. Payne."

But on the Labor and Delivery floor, we both stopped, awed at the sight of all the babies you could see through the nursery windows.

ALLI

I pushed open the door of room 226 and tiptoed inside. Mimi lay sprawled out on a recliner chair, snoring, her white hair mussed and mouth slightly open. And Mandy lay pale, under a blue blanket. Her eyes fluttered open.

Then shut.

She was still asleep.

I tiptoed to the bassinet beside her bed.

And there she was.

Baby was wide awake, looking around. Soft blond hair–almost invisible! Gently, almost afraid, I held out a finger and wrapped her fingers over it.

Baby held on and watched me, and I let the wonder and joy of Baby fill me. She knew me, recognized me. My little sister. I knew this was the only time I would see her, so I didn't move, just watched her tiny face. Leaned close to smell her. Baby oil, baby milk, sweet baby breath—I wanted to kiss her forehead, but dared not.

When I straightened, I saw the name on the card: Emily Elizabeth Payne.

It was the name I had suggested so long ago, the day we bought the schoolhouse quilt for the baby.

"No," Mandy had said, "Ted likes the name, Marianne."

I'm glad they hadn't named her that! Baby was definitely not a Marianne, not with those blond curls.

Watching Baby–no, her name was Emily—look around, blink, look around, I didn't think the sun could shine any brighter or my heart be any fuller. Emily Payne. My sister.

"What are you doing here?" Mandy demanded.

She pushed a button and tilted her bed up, wincing as she pushed up to sit. Her cheeks were fatter, and her hair was limp.

"I wanted to see her. Just once."

"You can't come back. Not ever."

"I know, Ted will be mad."

Mandy took a deep breath, and her jaw tightened. "You need to understand. Ted didn't send you away. I did. I had to."

I stared, not understanding.

"Ted was adopted as a baby, but he didn't find out until he was fifteen years old. It hurt him so deeply, he swore he would never adopt. But you tempted him; he liked you."

I wanted to plug my ears, to stop listening. But Emily still held my finger.

"But I knew that if he would just wait," Mandy's voice continued, "we would have our own child."

It was Mandy who sent me away, not Ted. Mandy who had decided that only her own child could be loved by her husband.

Ted had answered the phone that once, but I hadn't given him a chance to say anything. And that conversation I overheard right after the accident, I tried to think what exactly they said. And I heard Mandy's voice echoing, "You never wanted to adopt. Alli was only supposed to be here until we had our own baby."

It was Mandy all along. Or was it?

"But Ted had my phone calls blocked."

"He didn't know about that. I just called his friend, Derrick, at the office and asked him to do it. Ted kept wondering why you didn't call and ask about the baby."

I started to cry now, remembering the hot air balloon flights, the hours that Ted and I spent in the quiet sky, surrounded by clouds and dreams and hopes.

Emily whimpered, and I looked down at her tiny fingers and tiny fingernails.

"You have to understand. I can't let you interfere with our baby. With Emily."

Mandy had hopes and dreams, too. But her dreams were all so small, the dreams of a person with a small heart.

Oh! I had had a dad and didn't even know it. Never had a mom. My real mom died when I was born, and Mandy had never really loved me; her with a heart so small she couldn't let in another child. Even at the Porters, there was no mom. Eliot was right to help me search for my real dad.

Through my tears, I said, "It's okay. I won't bother you ever again."

Then the door opened again. I expected the nurse. Quickly, before anyone could stop me, I bent and kissed Emily's forehead. "I love you, sister," I said.

Then I straightened up.

The room was full, everyone staring at me: Mr. and Miss Porter, both frowning; Miss Brodie-Rock, talking to Ted; Mrs. Winston, looking solemn, and Eliot, looking sad. Mimi sat up suddenly, disoriented, and looked around wildly, calling, "What's going on?"

Then, everyone started talking at once, yelling and making a huge fuss.

"Shhhh!" I said it as loud as I could. As I did, my finger pulled away from Emily's tiny hand.

Startled, everyone looked at me and the bassinet.

And Emily let out a huge wail. Then took a breath and wailed again. "Waaaa, Waaaa!"

And I sank to the floor beside her bassinet and cried, too.

When the nurse arrived a few minutes later and chased everyone out, it was Ted who pulled me up. Wrapped his arm around my shoulder and walked with me, silent, toward the waiting room. But Miss Brodie-Rock and the Porters were waiting for us.

The fluorescent lights turned Mr. Porter's face a muddy gray. He started to talk, "Why did you think you could get away–"

Ignoring the Porters, I shook free of Ted and walked to the chairs where I had slept. I sat and started tying on my shoes.

Ted followed me and motioned for the others to stay away.

"What did you think of Emily?"

Bent over still, I nodded up at him. "Beautiful."

"So are you, Alli."

I turned away, angry now, jerked my backpack open and started brushing my hair.

Ted bent his head and held his hands together. "You're right, I shouldn't say that. There's no excuse for how we've hurt you. But Mandy was jealous, afraid. She wanted Emily to be the most important person in our lives. I shouldn't have agreed to let you go."

It was too late: events couldn't be unmade, I thought. I'd been set adrift among the clouds and would have to find my own bearings, steer my own way clear. But I saw now that there was a way through. Though Ted hadn't been able to finish what he'd started, to be my real dad, at least I saw something of what a father could be. Ted had given me hope. And for that gift alone, I was willing to forgive him.

Shouldering my backpack, I stood. Though I spoke to Ted, I turned to look at Miss Brodie-Rock. "I understand. But what's done is done. Go on. Emily needs you to be there. Just be there for her, for the rest of her life. If you can do that, it's okay. Just be there."

I saw Eliot standing beside Mrs. Winston, her hand on his shoulder. He nodded, he understood. And I nodded back.

Then, I walked over to Miss Brodie-Rock, put my hand into hers and looked up. "I'm ready."

And I looked behind just once, just long enough to see Ted walking down the hall toward his daughter, Emily.

ELIOT

Sunday was all sadness and wishes.

I wished I had been able to tell Alli goodbye. Instead, Miss Brodie-Rock had grabbed hold of her arm and held on tight, steering her onto the elevator. Alli didn't resist; there was no need. She had what she had wanted so much, to see Baby and to touch Baby and to make sure Baby was perfect, to see that Mandy's fall hadn't hurt Baby.

I wished that sadness about Alli didn't weigh so heavily on me as I measured flour, kneaded dough, played cards with Toby, and wished that Alli was here to eat a warm slice of sourdough bread, to watch me wrap the second loaf to take to the Thanksgiving dinner.

I watched Marj knead and braid a variation of our sourdough recipe. She was making extra loaves, in case there weren't enough at the auction. She didn't say I was in her way, but she didn't really do much to encourage me sitting there, either, except look up and smile. Twice she started to say something, but always stopped with a slight shake of her head.

I wished time didn't run so fast. But the days went by in a blink until there we were, on Tuesday morning, loading up and leaving for school, heading to the Thanksgiving dinner, the end of the Bread Project.

And I wished Alli was going with us.

THE BREAD PROJECT

ELIOT

Tuesday morning, the morning of the PTA Thanksgiving dinner, the sky had shrugged on a gray sweatshirt: it would rain later, and if it got cold enough, maybe sleet. Marj didn't make me go to school. Instead, we went together about 10 a.m. to help the Johnsons decorate.

Sharp metallic echoes filled the auditorium: parents setting up tables and chairs. Marj went to help Mrs. Lopez, Mrs. Johnson and Mrs. Patel carry in the cookbooks and set them up to sell. I helped Mr. Johnson roll out long sheets of green plastic to cover the tables, then tape them in place. Others came behind us, decorating with autumn leaves, pumpkins and such stuff. Someone had brought scented candles. Toby and I lit them, and soon, a spicy-sweet smell filled the air. Along each side wall, we helped set up other tables as serving lines for the food, which was in huge aluminum pans, just waiting to be uncovered when it was time to eat. Other tables were for the silent auction of breads–if we had too many loaves to auction in a reasonable time. The cafeteria slowly transformed from the cold concrete block room into a dining room full of light and laughter, blocking out the gray weather.

Everyone was chattering about holiday plans. Mr. Johnson was telling about leaving tomorrow for Chicago to see his mother. Mr. Patel explained that relatives from India were arriving that evening. Even Mr. Benton, who had stopped in to check our progress, was flying to Florida for a couple days on the beach. In the midst of this holiday bustle and cheer, I felt frozen. Because on the stage, we set up ten tables for the bread.

Finally, the room was ready.

Mrs. Lopez turned on the microphone and asked all the volunteers to gather in front of the stage for last minute instructions. The Herats were there, Mrs. Herat standing close to her husband so he could translate for her. She was obviously shy, but from the middle of her *burkha*, her dark eyes were bright and eager. The blond heads of Mr. and Mrs. Zane bounced through the crowd, their voices rising above others, as usual. A group of Hispanics in bright colored shirts was chattering in Spanish, while a couple of Egyptians fathers in casual khakis and school t-shirts stood back with crossed arms and just watched. I sat on the edge of the stage, kicking my legs, wondering if Heaven would be like this, with people from so many different nations. Wondering: where was Alli today, what family was she living with, and was it a good family for her? Wondering if Marj–who stood in the middle of the crowd–was pleased with the Bread Project she had set into motion so many weeks ago.

Finally Mrs. Lopez called for attention and explained the process for the next hour. "When people come in, send them to the stage first with their bread. We have a card to fill out, asking who made the bread and what kind of bread it is. Then, they can find a place to sit."

In a brilliant orange sari, Mrs. Patel leaned into the microphone to add, "Make sure the kids go with the parents and help fill it out. We have several families who don't read much English."

Then it was all ready.

It was time.

Ten empty tables waited to be filled with bread. Or not. And the overflow tables for silent auction if there were more loaves than we expected. If a bread went there, it would have a lined page for people to write their names and bids. People could come back as often as they wanted to up their bids. At the end of the night, the highest bidder on the page would take home that bread.

The procession of bread began. Clusters of families crowded onto the stage to register their breads, coming and going, filling up the auditorium. And the breads: *Pan dolce*, *ciabatti*, *ekmek*, *naan*, pretzels, *poori*, *pita* – my head swam with the names. The humble wheat grain was utterly transformed by human creativity into such a variety of forms. English muffins, raisin bread, cinnamon rolls, Kaiser rolls, potato rolls. Loaves of rye breads, whole wheat breads, just plain white loaves. *Focaccia*. Dutch

Crunch. Everything from A to Z: Anadama to Zucchini-Carob Bread.

Filling the auction tables at the front. And—what a surprise— even filling the silent auction tables around the room.

Somehow, in the swirl of it all, I found myself staring at Marj, her freckled face flushed as she stood at the side of the stage, holding one finger in her ear and her cell phone to her other ear. She was talking, nodding. Smiling.

Grissini, chleb, bolillo.

The bread tables were nearly full, and only a few people were still standing on the stage, waiting to register their breads. It was almost time to eat.

Marj turned and saw me. Over the hubbub, I raised my hands, asking who had called. Still smiling, she circled around to stand beside me and talk in my ear.

"That was Miss Clay. She just got a full price offer on the house."

Oh. A full price offer. I knew I should be either sad or glad, but I was just numb. I turned, still studying the variety of breads.

Brioche, bagels.

Bruschetta al pomodore.

Before I could say anything back to Marj, Mr. Benton was at the microphone calling for attention. It was time to serve the food. He turned and motioned for Marj and me to step up beside him.

I know he introduced us, and I waved at the crowd. But all I could think of was our home. And the full price offer. Mr. Benton said a few things about Griff and a few more things about Thanksgiving and being grateful and such. Then motioned for the serving to begin.

And Marj was guiding me down the steps toward the food tables. "Did you get a count of the breads?" she asked.

I shook my head. "Lots. That's all I know."

She smiled, a sad smile. "Griff would have loved all this. I wish he could have seen it."

To avoid that thought, I half-turned to where Mrs. Lopez and Mrs. Zane rushed around the stage taking stock of the breads. "Do they need help?"

"No. They didn't want any help for that. We'll just eat." She hesitated, "And maybe talk?"

A full price offer. At least my eyes were dry.

"Hey! There you are!" Toby slapped my back. He wore an orange T-shirt, just like his parents – big surprise. "Come on, I saved you a place." He motioned to a group of the guys standing in the line on the other side of the room and asked Marj, "You don't mind if he sits with us?"

Marj stepped back slightly. "Go on, I'll sit with some other moms. We'll talk later."

Toby started walking away, "Hey, Eliot, how many different breads are there? Did you count?"

"Later," I murmured to Marj and followed Toby.

Toby was hungry, as usual. He sat across the green plastic tablecloth from me, Sam beside him, and other guys around us. We filled a whole table by ourselves. And we stuffed ourselves, even going back for a second helping of everything—the turkey, dressing, green beans, cranberry sauce and pumpkin pie had been catered, not cooked in the school cafeteria.

There was a clamor by the back door, and a TV reporter and cameraman came in, Channel 5. I leaned back and looked around. The room was stuffed with people. But I realized there were some people missing.

First, I hadn't seen Mr. Porter. Maybe he would quit teaching after this year; he never seemed happy anyway.

Second, we had invited the Mayor and all the councilmen, the superintendent and all the school board. The Mayor was missing for sure, and that probably meant few councilmen had come either, except Mr. Zane. And I couldn't find the superintendent, which meant few school board members were here either, except our zone's representative, Mr. Rice, a man I had only seen but never met. Mr. Benton had talked to the PTA about getting publicity for this event, but Thanksgiving holiday had too many other events.

It all made me worry a little. Who would buy all that bread?

The committee had said it was like old-fashioned pie suppers, that families would bid on their own bread. Would we make any money? This wasn't the richest part of Nashville.

On stage, Mrs. Lopez turned on the mike and blew, but no noise came out. Coming over, Mrs. Zane tried moving the ON switch on the back of the mike, but still nothing. She shrugged, then put her fingers to her mouth and whistled. Wheeeee!

The room was suddenly silent. I knew everyone was thinking, Zany Zanes. But I was remembering that Alli called Mrs. Zane, the Mighty Whistler. It was sad to be here without Alli.

Mrs. Zane yelled, "Anyone know how to get the microphone working? It's almost time for the Bread Auction."

Mr. Benton and a couple teachers trotted to the stage to recheck the equipment. Meanwhile, chairs scraped as people turned to face the stage. Finally, Mr. Benton tapped the microphone, and it screeched. After a few more minutes testing, they decided it was fixed.

Mrs. Zane stepped to the microphone. "We have counted the breads. There are 493 students registered at the school, as of today. And we have 576 different breads! Thank all of you for helping to make this happen."

She paused for the clapping and cheering to quiet. Then: "The PTA has voted to donate all the proceeds from this auction to the school for playground equipment." She explained how the silent auction worked at the tables around the room. Then, she pointed to a table near the door where Mrs. Patel was holding up a book. "And don't forget to buy a cookbook as you leave!"

Mrs. Lopez, the Mouth, as Alli called her, was the auctioneer. That figured.

"It's time to sell, sell, sell some bread. We'll auction 50 breads from here while you walk around and do the silent auctions. *Amigos*, you'll want to sample the bread from someone else, don't bid *solamente*, only, on your own family's bread. With all these kinds of bread," she waved at the tables behind her, "you'll have a treat for Thanksgiving."

From the crowd, especially the little kids, there came a faint cry, "Bread, bread. Hurray for bread!"

But I turned triumphantly to Toby. "576!"

Toby shook his head, his straight blond hair swinging. "You called it." He pulled out his billfold. But for once, he didn't have enough. "Only $40. I owe you ten."

"Don't worry about it." I was glad to have this much for my nest egg since I would be moving to a new family next weekend.

Onstage, Mrs. Zane said, "Good luck with the bidding. Remember, when you buy bread today, you are really buying a piece of fun for your child."

Mrs. Lopez nodded. And this time, she really started the auctioneer's patter, the sing-song, "Who'll give me a dollar, a dollar, a dollar, who'll start the bidding at a dollar for this package of large, fresh pretzels? Looks like de-licious pretzels, delightful pretzels, who'll start the bidding for the Bread Auction."

The Channel 5 cameraman was down front filming Mrs. Lopez. And PTA people were standing around the room, ready to help.

But the room was silent.

No one was bidding. Nothing.

"Don't be shy, now. The first bid is the hardest. Who'll give me a dollar, five dollars, a dollar, five dollars, who'll start the bidding for the pretzels?"

Silence.

"This is for the playground equipment for your kids. *Por los muchachos y las muchachas*. They'll have a jungle gym, swings, a safe place to play. Who'll start the bidding? A dollar, a dollar, five dollars, a dollar."

My heart pounded as I looked at the money that Toby had just handed over, the crisp $5 bills. Griffith Winston was the finest man I had ever known, and this auction was a tribute to him. I should buy some bread. But that money was all I had to take with me when I had to go to a foster home. It was my hidden jar of peanut butter, my pair of socks with no holes, the only spending money I might have for anything that I would need.

Mrs. Lopez took another deep breath and her patter went on. "De-licious pretzel, a bargain at just a dollar. Who'll start the bidding? I know, you're shy, you don't want to be the first. Who'll start the bidding? *Solamente un dolar.*"

But then, other images filled my heart: Marj sitting in the sunny breakfast room with a bag of pretzels at her elbow, reading the newspaper. Yes, I missed Griff and always would. But somehow, without me noticing, Marj had filled the space that Griff had left behind, and I wanted to do one last thing for her. If it had been cinnamon rolls or English muffins, I would have done nothing. But pretzels? Big soft pretzels like they sold at the mall? Pretzels?

I stood up. Sit down, I told myself.

I opened my mouth. Shut up, I told myself.

I took a deep breath and called as loud as I could. "$40. I bid $40."

Mrs. Lopez paused and looked at me.

With her white teeth shining in her dark face, a broad smile lit her up, and the auctioneer's patter took on an intensity. "$40, I have a bid of $40 for these pretzels. Do I hear $41? $45? $50? I have a bid of $40. De-lightful pretzels, bid of $40. Who'll go $45?"

Everyone was looking at me.

Toby's mouth hung open, and he leaned over like he might snatch the cash away. The Herats, the Patels, the Johnsons—everyone stared. Startled, I realized that in the back of the room was the red-haired woman I had talked to at the Community Center. And with her were more faces I recognized from the Community Center, including the bald man with the strong aftershave and the skinny man who smelled like he never bathed. They had come and I hadn't even realized it.

"I have a bid of $40. Going once. Do I hear $45?"

Still looking around, Marj's face popped out at me. Pale, but her chin was up, defiant, and maybe a bit proud. Not smiling, but that was OK. She didn't go overboard in smiles.

"Going twice. Do I hear $45?"

On stage, Mrs. Zane held up the clear sack that was stuffed with soft pretzels. Mrs. Lopez gave me a thumbs-up.

Mrs. Lopez's gavel banged. "Sold! To Mr. Eliot Winston, a true son of the ever-generous Griffith Winston, for $40."

And around the room a cheer rang out.

I walked to the front and was shepherded to a PTA table to pay. Behind me Mrs. Lopez started next bidding—for Polish *chleb*—at $10, and three voices jumped right in. Startled, I looked around: the Community Center redhead, Mr. Patel, and another Hispanic father were bidding. For a loaf of Polish bread. I almost laughed out loud. Only at this school, in this community, would you see such a thing.

After fierce bidding, the price going up a single dollar at a time, the *chleb* went for $25. Finished paying, I walked across the room to Marj. I set the pretzels on the table in front of her and smiled. She said nothing, but her eyes were shining. I don't know what she was thinking, but it didn't matter. It was what I wanted to do.

My money, my choice.

I nodded once, then turned and went back to Toby and the other guys.

The rest of the bidding was fast and furious and decisive, with nothing going for under $20. Even the silent auction breads went for at least $10 each. The Bread Project was a spectacular success.

AFTER THE BREAD PROJECT

ELIOT

The sleet never came, just cold, steady rains that kept us indoors on Wednesday. Marj took me to a movie that afternoon, and we snuck in four of the soft pretzels to eat: three for Marj and one for me. Coming out of the movie theater, the rain was tapering off, but now it was foggy, hard to see very far.

Driving home, I was quiet, just letting Marj concentrate on driving in the fog. We didn't talk about the offer on the house. Marj didn't mention it, and I didn't ask. It was just a quiet, calm day. I guess we were both content to wait until the holiday was over to decide anything. Now that we were down to the last days of our agreement, I didn't want to push for answers. Waiting was better than knowing.

That evening on the TV news, Channel 5 ran a story on our Bread Project, and I was there, bidding $40. They even filmed me walking over to Marj and giving her the pretzels.

Mrs. Patel called right after, thrilled that the news report had mentioned the cookbooks and given an email address to order them. She had already gotten one order and hoped there would be more. The TV station said they would play the clip from the Bread Project several times that weekend—it was good community PR for the station—and surely they would get more cookbook orders. She said the Bread Project auction had brought in over $10,000. More than enough for the playground equipment, and they would have to talk about how to use the extra money.

Griff had been right: Any community could come together and do something spectacular.

Sometime that night, the skies cleared and a brisk wind blew, a comforting bluster around the sky light of my cockpit room, the winds drying things out so that Thanksgiving morning dawned clear and cold and dry.

I hadn't set the alarm, but I woke at 6 a.m., dressed and went down to the garage. The old push mower was sharp and oiled, and I took it out one last time to mow the backyard. It barely needed it; the grass barely grew in the cold. But I wanted to use Griff's tools one last time. The snick, snick, snick of the rolling lawnmower blades pleased me.

By the time I went in, Marj was in the kitchen cooking. My stomach did a flip because surely, we would talk today. Maybe after the dinner was done and cleaned up. Surely, Marj wouldn't keep putting it off, wouldn't wait until tomorrow. I was starting to get anxious, wanting to know now what would happen.

Meanwhile, we watched the Thanksgiving parades on TV and cooked. Cranberry sauce from fresh cranberries. Roasted Cornish hens–we had agreed that a turkey was too big. Baked sourdough French bread loaves, one of the recipes from the new cookbook. Corn on the cob. Baked potatoes. While we cooked, we snacked on the last of the soft pretzels.

"I'll have to make some of these myself next week," Marj said.

I set the table, shaking out a tablecloth and using the best china and real silverware. The crystal glasses, I filled with sparkling grape juice. When everything was ready, we sat down to eat. On TV, the parades were all done and football games had started. Marj flipped to an old movie, It's a Wonderful Life, and left it on with a low volume while we ate.

I remembered how Griff had filled the eating time with talk and laughter; now it seemed normal to eat and enjoy the food without much talking.

Finally, Marj pushed away her plate. "That was great. We'll have to have Cornish hens again next year."

Startled, I looked up. "Next year?" My pulse pounded.

"We need to talk," she said.

"Yes."

"Where do we go from here?"

I started to just ask where she wanted to go from here. But. Alli had said I needed to talk to Marj, to communicate. I just needed to be myself, she had said.

I drew a shaky breath. "I'm scared. I don't know if we can be a real family together. But I want to try."

Marj's shoulders sagged a bit. "I'm so glad you said that because I'm scared, too."

"I know I have lots of problems, but I'm trying to stop the panic attacks. I'm trying–"

"Oh, Eliot. I know that. It's not about your problems. It's about how ignorant I am of being a parent. I'm just not good at this."

That was all crazy. "You've been great. I know I got mad that day you were late, but I was so scared 'cause the panic attacks had come back."

"And I forget to give you allowances, so you have to make bets with Toby."

"You figured that out?" I hardly dared look at her.

"Finally."

I stared at my plate, still scared to look up.

"Eliot. Eliot Winston," she said softly.

Still without looking up, I said, "I called you at the office last Friday." I was so scared to tell her what I was thinking. So tired of being scared.

"You did?"

"I almost had a panic attack at school, but I kept control. Miss Clay let me call."

"That's great that you kept control," she said. Then, puzzled, "But I didn't talk to you that day."

"No. I talked to Miss Street. She said you had just gone out to talk to a social worker and to see Mr. Donovan. And now, you have a full price offer on the house. And the Bread Project is over, so our agreement is over."

"I didn't know you had called." She ran a hand over her eyes. "I just wanted to wait until Thanksgiving Day."

Now, suddenly, I had to know. "Just tell me. Am I going to stay or go?"

"Eliot Winston."

Now I did look up. Marj's hair was pulled back into a short ponytail, growing out long again. Her face was skinny and pale, but she didn't have dark circles under her eyes like she had early that fall. She was leaning over the best china and real silverware toward me.

She said, "I'm scared. Scared that I'll mess up. But—" She picked up a piece of the sourdough bread. "—families are like bread: they take a lot of time and patience. The Bread Project has been amazing. I've never felt so connected to a community. I knew Griff always felt that way, whatever community he was in, but I never did. And I know that Griff knew how to fight for the people he loved. But I've never known that, either. Even after he's gone, he's still teaching me about community and people and family."

I said nothing. Just waited. Because she still hadn't answered the question.

Marj drew a deep breath. "I went and talked to the social worker last week and told her that I wanted you to stay with me. I talked to Mr. Donovan and told him that I'd sign the papers this week and get them back to him on Monday. But I wanted to give you the choice, too. It's not just my decision. I want you to stay. But what do you want?"

I remembered Alli's harsh voice yelling at me. "You have a chance. A chance for a real family. You have to fight for your family."

It was the second chance that I thought I'd never get.

Hesitantly, I said, "Mom?"

And she stood and took a step toward me, "Eliot Winston. Come here, Son."

And I took the step that closed the gap, and she wrapped her skinny arms around me in the biggest hug ever.

Friday morning, the skies were golden, like someone had poured melted butter on the few remaining clouds. During breakfast, I explained about renting the post office box for Alli and asked if we could go to see if there were any letters. Walking into the old building, I saw a sparrow hopping on the floor. I held open the door, and Marj circled the sparrow and shooed it toward the door. It didn't fly up, even though it was a two-story foyer. Instead, it hopped away from her as I stood outside, holding the door so the bird couldn't see me. And then it hopped outside. It shook its tail feathers once, hopped again, then launched into the clear blue skies.

Inside, I found PO Box 491, a golden bronze door, just at eye-height. Just like Alli had said it would be. The door unlocked with a slight click. And there were two letters.

"Who from?" Marj asked.

"Alli!" I tore open the one with her handwriting.

> "Dear Eliot:
>
> Let me tell you right off, this new place is good."

She was only ten miles way and the new foster home had two girls. Alli had new clothes, and plenty to eat and a big sister and a little sister. I handed the letter to Mom to read.

"She gives her phone number. Do you want to call her later?"

I nodded and turned the other letter over in my hands. It was just a standard business size envelope, addressed to Alli at this PO box, but there was no return address. I opened it and read:

> "Dear Alli:
>
> I don't know if I am the person you are looking for or not. But I was in the US Army and when I came home, I couldn't find my wife or mother-in-law or daughter. She was born on. . ."

Included was a picture of a soldier taken with his daughter at Wal-Mart right before he left on tour. It was the same picture that Alli had carried for years.

Alli's Dad.

We could call Alli, Marj said, and take the letter over to her.

I agreed, but first I had something to show Marj. When we got home, I took a deep breath and asked Marj to come upstairs to my room, and I had her sit in a chair beside my computer desk. And I pulled up the website I had made for Griffith Winston, Dad and Husband. We clicked through the pictures and read the stories that people from the community center and other places had sent me.

And we cried for what we had lost.

And for what we had gained.

ABOUT THE AUTHOR

Translated into eight languages, children's book author **DARCY PATTISON** writes picture books, middle grade novels, and children's nonfiction. Previous titles include *The Journey of Oliver K. Woodman* (Harcourt), *Searching for Oliver K. Woodman* (Harcourt), *The Wayfinder* (Greenwillow), *19 Girls and Me* (Philomel), *Prairie Storms* (Sylvan Dell), *Desert Baths* (Desert Baths), and *Wisdom, the Midway Albatross* (Mims House.) Her work has been recognized by *starred reviews* in *Kirkus*, *BCCB*, and *PW*. *Desert Baths* was named a 2013 Outstanding Science Trade Book and the *Library Media Connection*, Editor's Choice. She is a member of the Society of Children's Bookwriters and Illustrators and the Author's Guild. For more information, see
darcypattison.com OR mimshouse.com

Join our mailing list: MimsHouse.com/newsletter/

OTHER BOOKS BY DARCY PATTISON

Saucy and Bubba: A Hansel and Gretel Tale
The Girl, the Gypsy and the Gargyole
Vagabonds
Abayomi, the Brazilian Puma:
Wisdom, the Midway Albatross:
Searching for Oliver K. Woodman
The Journey of Oliver K. Woodman
I Want a Dog: My Opinion Essay
I Want a Cat: My Opinion Essay
The Aliens, Inc. Series
- ***Book 1: Kell, the Alien***
- ***Book 2: Kell and the Horse Apple Parade***
- ***Book 3: Kell and the Giants***
- ***Book 4: Kell and the Detectives***